Pictorial History of

AUSTRALIA'S LITTLE CORNWALL

Philip Payton is Professor of History at Flinders University in Adelaide, and Emeritus Professor of Cornish & Australian Studies at the University of Exeter in the UK, where he was Director of the Institute of Cornish Studies from 1991 to 2013. He is the author/editor of more than fifty books, including *Making Moonta: The Invention of 'Australia's Little Cornwall'* (2007) and *Regional Australia and the Great War: 'The Boys from Old Kio'* (2012), both of which are about the history of northern Yorke Peninsula.

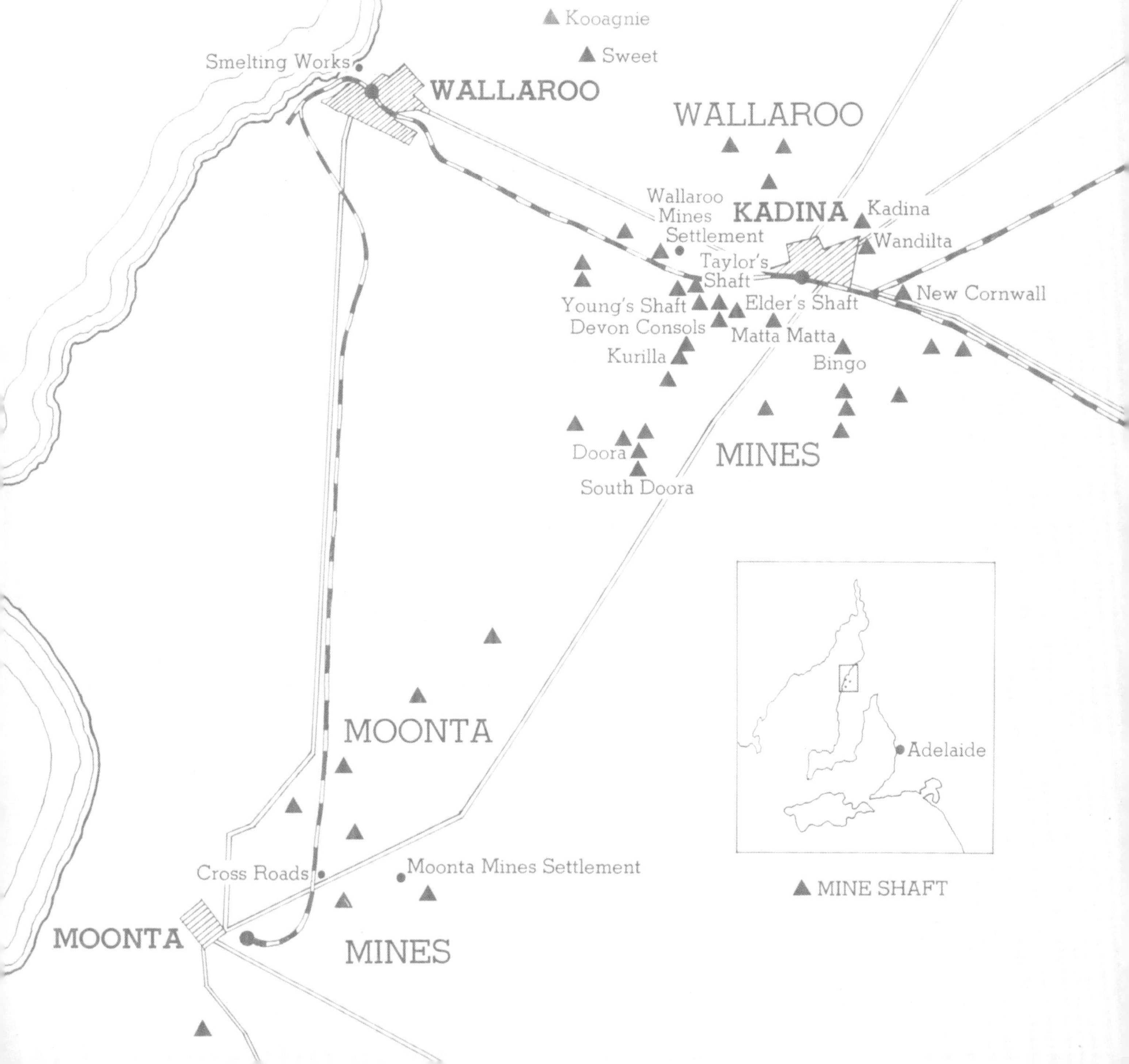

Kooagnie
Sweet
Smelting Works
WALLAROO
WALLAROO
Wallaroo Mines Settlement
KADINA
Kadina
Wandilta
Taylor's Shaft
New Cornwall
Young's Shaft
Elder's Shaft
Devon Consols
Matta Matta
Kurilla
Bingo
Doora
MINES
South Doora
MOONTA
Adelaide
Cross Roads
Moonta Mines Settlement
MINE SHAFT
MOONTA
MINES

Pictorial History of AUSTRALIA'S LITTLE CORNWALL

Philip Payton

Wakefield Press

Wakefield Press
16 Rose Street
Mile End
South Australia 5031
www.wakefieldpress.com.au

First published 1978
This edition published 2020

Cover designed by Liz Nicholson, Wakefield Press
Text designed and typeset by Wakefield Press
Printing and quality control in China by Tingleman Pty Ltd

ISBN 978 1 74305 655 4

NATIONAL LIBRARY OF AUSTRALIA
A catalogue record for this book is available from the National Library of Australia

CORIOLE McLAREN VALE
Wakefield Press thanks Coriole Vineyards for continued support

To the memory of my grandfather, Cecil Williams, Cornishman and engineer.

Frontispiece: Moonta Mines – one of the finest examples of Cornish mining architecture to be found in Australia *(photo by Evelyn Low).*

Below: Wyatt's classic sketch of the Moonta Mines in 1862. Elder's Shaft was the first to be sunk on what came to be known as 'Elder's and Taylor's Main Lode', situated almost a kilometre east of where Patrick Ryan first discovered copper in 1861. In the centre of the sketch is a horse whim equipped with two ropes – one for hauling the kibble up the shaft, and the other for letting it down. A little to the left of the whim is a whip, a device by means of which a horse hauls a kibble from shallow workings. In the bottom left-hand corner are what appear to be boilers, and scattered around the area is the characteristic deep-flanged pit-work piping – an indication that an engine is about to be erected.

Contents

Preface 7
Acknowledgments 9
Foreword 10
Introduction 12
Prelude 27
The Wallaroo Mines 29
Settlements: Kadina and Wallaroo Mines 39
The Moonta Mines 47
Settlements: Moonta and Moonta Mines 53
The Smaller Mining Ventures 61
Settlements: Wallaroo and its Smelting Works 67
Cousin Jack Underground 75
Chapels, Banners and Bands 83
The Years of Change 91
Bibliography 96

Preface

More than forty years ago, as I struggled to complete my PhD thesis on 'The Cornish in South Australia' at the University of Adelaide, I stumbled across a large collection of historic photographs in the Archives section of the State Library. These wonderful photographs, I soon discovered, vividly depicted everyday life in the late nineteenth and early twentieth-century copper mines, smelters and mining communities of Moonta, Wallaroo and Kadina on northern Yorke Peninsula, an area known collectively as 'Australia's Little Cornwall'.

As well as being struck by their originality and significance, I felt strongly that these images should be brought to life beyond the Archives and drawn to the attention of as wide an audience as possible, perhaps in an illustrated book where the photographs could be accompanied by an historical narrative and given extensive captions that would provide context and explanations. It was the beginning of my enthusiasm for 'popular' history, of bringing the fruits of scholarly research out of the purely academic sphere (universities and the like) and presenting them in accessible form to the broader community, a life-long enthusiasm that is with me still.

Today such an approach is known in higher education circles as 'impact', and is applauded by universities which seek to foster and encourage such 'outreach' activities. Back in 1978, however, eyebrows were raised by such a radical suggestion, and it was to his great credit that my then supervisor, the late Dr John Playford, readily saw my point and recommended that I approach Rigby Ltd, the Adelaide publishers, with a book proposal. Rigby, to my delight, was also taken with the idea, and thus the *Pictorial History of Australia's Little Cornwall* was born, appearing in November 1978 when I was twenty-four years old and on the eve of submitting my PhD.

Pictorial History of Australia's Little Cornwall achieved favourable reviews in both Cornwall and Australia, and even won a modest prize in an ANZ Bank local history competition in 1979. But, as is the way with books, it gradually fell out of print, becoming more difficult to find (and expensive to buy) on the second-hand market. Over the years, friends periodically urged me to organise a reprint or second edition, notably Liz Coole, doyenne of Moonta's local historians, and the late Jim Harbison OAM - both Cornish bards - as did fellow members of the Cornish Association of South Australia, including the late Roslyn Paterson OAM (another Cornish bard) who had written the Foreword to the first edition.

Left: The 'Copper Centenary', held in Moonta in 1961, commemorated the discovery of the Moonta Mines a century earlier; and as part of the celebrations a memorial (a detail of which is shown here) was erected in memory of the Cornish miners who gave their lives to the industry. The complete memorial is shown on page 97. A similar centenary had been held a year earlier at Kadina, Wallaroo, and Wallaroo Mines.

The idea of a reprint remained something of a pipe-dream until the Moonta Branch of the National Trust of South Australia, under the auspices of Stephen Stock OAM, decided that it would sponsor a new edition of the *Pictorial History of Australia's Little Cornwall* in response to the National Heritage Listing for Moonta Mines announced by the Commonwealth Government in May 2017. Building upon existing State heritage listings, both Burra and Moonta Mines, seen as exemplars of South Australia's historic Cornish mining landscapes, had been selected as the 109th and 110th places to be added to the National Heritage List, recognition of their national and international significance, and a prelude to an application to UNESCO for World Heritage Site status in which they would be linked to the Cornish mining landscapes of Cornwall and West Devon, which had been granted such status in 2006.

Following negotiations between Moonta National Trust and Wakefield Press publisher, Michael Bollen, this second edition of *Pictorial History of Australia's Little Cornwall* came into being, a little more than forty years since the first edition had appeared. Needless to say, I am deeply grateful to both organisations for their enthusiasm for this project, and am delighted to see the book in print again at such a timely moment.

I have avoided making major changes to the original text, and have restricted myself to correcting obvious errors. I have allowed various naiveties to stand, though they make me smile today, and I have continued to tolerate the editorial interventions of the original publishers, even though they still cause me to wince. Although written in what we thought were the progressive 1970s - the heady days of Don Dunstan's premiership in South Australia - the book is in some ways a child of its time. I have used 'Cornishmen', for instance, as a generic term for both Cornish men and women, when today I would have been far more gender-specific as well as anxious to emphasise the important role of women - of Cousin Jenny as well as Cousin Jack - in what was at first glance a male-oriented culture of mining, wrestling, brass bands and male-voice choirs. Likewise, I am sorry that I did not mention the early contacts between Cornish settlers and the indigenous Narungga people, despite then having to hand the report to the Royal Geological Society of Cornwall by Captain Samuel Higgs of Wallaroo Mines in 1875 in which he confessed that 'I am not inclined to speak so disparagingly of the aborigines as the writers of some books are: I see pretty much of them, and find them to be shrewd observers, with a great fund of humour, and inimitable caricaturists'.

Generally, however, reviewing again the text and captions after all these years, I am surprised how well they stand up with the passage of time. They remain, I hope, along with the extraordinary collection of illustrations they describe, a valuable insight into a colourful and economically, socially and politically significant region of South Australia. Today it is gratifying that the people and places of 'Australia's Little Cornwall' are once again a focus of national and international attention.

Philip Payton,
Flinders University,
Adelaide, South Australia

Acknowledgments

This book was undertaken largely at the suggestion, and through the encouragement, of Dr John Playford and it is to him that acknowledgment is due principally. Special thanks is also due to Roslyn Paterson whose splendid hospitality, enthusiasm for Cornish history, and willingness to introduce me to the people and places of 'Little Cornwall' combined to provide the ideal conditions in which to pursue the fieldwork necessary for this project.

I am also indebted to various other people and institutions for their help and advice - to Ian Auhl for his invaluable suggestions and assistance; to Mr and Mrs Jan Thomas and Rose Tripp for their colourful reminiscences of 'old-time' Moonta; to Perc Chynoweth for his information concerning the Wallaroo smelting works; to Gill Rosewarne for details of the Rosewarne family history; to the Kadina Branch of the National Trust of South Australia for permission to examine and use its historical material; and to John Cowling for allowing me access to the autobiography of Thomas Cowling.

I must also acknowledge the assistance rendered by the State Library of South Australia - the Reference Services Section, the South Australian Collection, the Newspaper Reading Room, the Photographic Section, the Sales Office, and particularly the Archives, whose helpful and friendly staff have made research a smooth and pleasant task. Thanks, too, must go to the equally helpful staff of the Barr Smith Library of the University of Adelaide, and to Mrs P. Canty, Librarian at the Parkin Wesley College.

The photographs in this book are reproduced by kind permission of the Archives Section of the State Library, except where otherwise stated when acknowledgment is due to Miss P. Minhard and to the Publicity Branch of the Premier's Department, State Government of South Australia, for allowing me to reproduce items from their respective photographic collections.

A word of thanks should also go to the countless individuals who over the years have deposited historic photographs in the State Archives for posterity and the benefit of research workers, and to the photographers and artists themselves whose foresight prompted them to record scenes which would otherwise have been lost for ever-one such photographer, Reg White, lives still in retirement at Wallaroo Mines.

Philip Payton,
University of Adelaide, 1978

Foreword

From that picturesque Celtic land called Cornwall, the Cornish miners and their families who emigrated to Australia brought with them not only their knowledge of mining, but also their unique customs, music, dialect, and even a smattering of Kernewek, the Cornish language.

They came to the dry, undulating country of Yorke Peninsula - a waterless area bereft of creeks, rivers or springs with only mallee and acacia trees and bushes covering the landscape. My own ancestor, Walter Phillips, with three other Cornish miners tested the first shaft on Yorke Peninsula at Wallaroo Mines in 1860. Just twelve months later the neighbouring Moonta Mines were established which, after an eventful beginning, developed into a bonanza for their owners.

Over the years, since those initial heady days in 1860 when copper was first mined, the residents of northern Yorke Peninsula have always been aware that they are a little different from the many other settlers in South Australia. May Vivienne, in her book *Sunny South Australia*, published in 1908, said that 'the people living there have a very high opinion of themselves - which I grant is a good thing to have'. When the mines and their associated industries collapsed, many Cornish people moved to Broken Hill, Kalgoorlie and Adelaide, but very many stayed and found work locally.

And what of the Cornish way of life that was so evident in the salad days of copper mining; does it still survive? The Cornish heritage is evident today in the various former Methodist churches still supported by people bearing names such as Rodda, Trengove, Polgreen, Thomas, Roberts and Hawke. Pasties complete with traditional crimping, saffron cakes and buns, and a vast array of sweet and savoury pies grace many a table.

Brass band music survives and choirs still sing 'Trelawney', Cornish carols, and 'The Cornish Floral Dance'. The remaining Cornish miners' cottages are cherished and much sought after.

And, above all, a growing interest in South Australia's Cornish heritage is evident. One important manifestation of this interest is the Kernewek Lowender Cornish festival, held biennially in oddnumbered years on the third weekend in May. Then, the people of 'Australia's Little Cornwall', living in the towns of Kadina, Moonta and Wallaroo, join together in celebrating their heritage with the Cornish Furry Dance, concerts, church services, a Cornish fair, and a proliferation of Cornish pasties. Kernewek Lowender is run by an executive of local people plus a general committee of approximately one hundred. These people recognise the need to preserve the Cornish heritage and the necessity of providing increased opportunities for the district's workforce. Unsponsored by big business, the festival has an attraction in its simplicity to the many thousands of Australians who have Cornish blood in their veins.

I hope very much that this book by Philip Payton will further extend and enhance this bourgeoning interest in the Cousin Jacks and Jennies of South Australia.

Roslyn M. Paterson
Bard of the Cornish Gorsedd, Akeringa, Willamulka

Below: Kadina township in 1862, already a sizeable community and able to boast several large and substantial buildings. This sketch has been attributed to W. Wyatt, who busied himself sketching various subjects drawn from the northern Yorke Peninsula mining scene.

Introduction

In South Australia today there can be few long-established families who cannot point to Cornish branches somewhere in their family trees; and the mark of the 'Cousin Jacks' - who came in such numbers in the last century - is to be found stamped indelibly upon the social, economic and political history of South Australia. Elsewhere in the world, particularly in North America and southern Africa, the distinctive contribution of the Cornish migrants can also be traced. For the Cornish were themselves a distinctive people. Cornwall had inherited the ancient Celtic tradition and this stood her apart from the Anglo-Saxon counties across the River Tamar border. Instead she shared a common heritage with the Welsh and Bretons.

Cornwall had her own Celtic language, similar to those of Wales and Brittany, which was spoken as a natural tongue until modern times. It lingered on into the twentieth century to be revitalised by the enthusiastic vanguard of the great Cornish Revival. Constitutionally, too, Cornwall was 'different'. Despite her ostensible administrative status as being just another British county, the Duchy of Cornwall (an institution linked with the Principality of Wales) gave her a unique relationship with the Crown. There was in addition a Stannary (or Tinners') Parliament, thus affording Cornwall a certain measure of theoretical political independence from London. Although the Parliament last met in the eighteenth century, its associated legal system of Stannary Courts continued to function until 1897.

In the nineteenth century many of the attributes of Cornish individualism remained, and Cornwall was recognised as a land apart by commentators on both sides of the Tamar, and by the ordinary Cornish folk themselves. Cornwall was known popularly as 'West Barbary', and there existed the saying 'into Cornwall, out of England'. To the Cornish, people from 'up-country' were automatically foreigners, and visitors to Cornwall often remarked on its un-English atmosphere. Writing in the 1860s, Wilkie Collins, the British novelist, reminded his readers that Cornwall was '. . . a county where, it must be remembered, a stranger is doubly a stranger, in relation to provincial sympathies; where the national feeling is almost entirely merged in the local feeling; where a man speaks of himself as CORNISH in much the same spirit as a Welshman speaks of himself as Welsh'.

In 1871 Robert Hunt, the folk-historian, noted that in Cornwall 'England, with many persons, appeared to terminate on the shores of the Tamar'. At the turn of this century, Henry Jenner - a Cornish scholar of considerable repute - could confidently claim that 'every Cornishman knows well enough, proud as he may be of belonging to the British Empire, that he is no more an Englishman than a Caithness man is, that he has as much right to a separate local patriotism to his little motherland . . . as has a Scotsman, an Irishman, a Welshman, or even a Colonial; and that he is as much a Celt and as little of an Anglo-Saxon as any Gael, Cymro, Manxman or Breton'.

Celtic customs and traditions persisted in nineteenth-century Cornwall, with Cornish wrestling featuring as a favourite sport and bonfires continuing to be lit on Midsummer's Eve, as they had been in ancient times. The Helston Furry Dance, with its Hal-an-Tow ceremony, was performed in May of every year, as was the Padstow Hobby Horse celebration. At St Columb Major the Celtic game of hurling continued to flourish, whilst elsewhere in Cornwall hurling matches survived until the early 1800s.

Despite this separate identity, Cornwall played a major role in Britain's Industrial Revolution and became established as one of the principal mining centres of the world. Although it is common to associate Cornwall with the production of tin, it was in fact copper mining which predominated in the nineteenth century, tin only being extracted on a large scale after the collapse of the Cornish copper industry in the late 1860s. Cornish mining was characterised, too, by its widely fluctuating fortunes, with periods of wealth and prosperity being followed all too often by depression and wholesale unemployment. Changing mineral prices, overseas competition (including ore from South Australia), and the long term structural decline of Cornish copper mining were all responsible for this volatile state of affairs.

Cornwall's other staple industries, farming and fishing, were also faced with periods of crippling depression. Although parts of Cornwall were well suited to agriculture, there were also great tracts of moorland and marginal country in which the Cornish farmer had to struggle to win a living from poor, acidic soil. High taxation and indifferent economic conditions combined with periodic crises (such as the potato blights in the 1840s) to force him off the land and overseas to new pastures. The Cornish fisherman fared little better, for he was involved in an industry which, despite years of high demand for Cornish seafood, was affected by long term decline which culminated, at the end of the century, in widespread collapse when 'Thousands of men . . . were thrown idle, their families hungry'.

It is not surprising, then, that emigration should have been such a feature of nineteenth-century Cornish history. In the latter two-thirds of the century Cornwall lost more than a third of her sons and daughters to new-found countries across the world. Just as the early period of the Industrial Revolution had seen a dramatic rise in the population of various Cornish mining parishes, so the years after 1840 bore witness to severe depopulation all over Cornwall.

South Australia was founded in 1836, in the first decade of what is termed Cornwall's 'Great Emigration'. Symbolically, the first adult male colonist to set foot on South Australian soil was Samuel Stephens, the son of a Cornish miner-preacher, who landed at Nepean Bay on Kangaroo Island on 27 July 1836. Within a few years he had been joined by literally hundreds of other Cornishmen, and in the period 1836 to 1840, ten per cent of all applications for free passage to South Australia were lodged in Cornwall.

Most of these were from working people, who were selected by the local migration agents. Typical of the early Cornish migrants were Samson Bastian, miner and husbandman of Tremaine, near Crowan; William Bennett, miner of Tolcarne Street, Camborne; Joseph Williams, a labourer from Carhays; William Vercoe, formerly a tailor in Truro; George Treverton, a Bodmin cobbler; Sampson Sanders, a mason from Tideford in St Germans parish; Joseph Julian, maltster and farmer from Ruan High Lanes; Sukey Fletcher, a bal-maiden (female mine worker) from Wheal Butson at St Agnes.

All this was in the years before South Australia's first mineral discoveries. The fact that South Australia was to be free of convict settlers, and would be colonised according to the rules of a pre-conceived system, was appealing to Cornish Methodist respectability; and the opportunity for individual improvement offered by emigration to a newly opened-up country also appealed to the Wesleyan self-help ethos which permeated Cornish society.

The 'Hungry Forties', which were as disastrous for Cornwall as they were for Ireland, also gave impetus to migration from Cornwall to South Australia. In 1845 and again in 1846 the Cornish potato crop was all but destroyed by the blight, and in 1847 William Allen, a migration agent at Penzance in the potato growing locality, noted that '. . . there is great excitement in this county and neighbourhood. Many persons in the Penzance district were preparing to emigrate to South Australia'. In 1849 nearly five per cent of the Penzance Union left for Australia and New Zealand, and in the following year fifty persons left the West Cornish farming parish of Mawgan-in-Meneage to come to South Australia.

Poverty in general promoted migration. Samuel Stanton, for instance, ran away from parish bondage (in which he had been placed as a child on the death of his parents) at St Cleer, near Liskeard, to migrate to New South Wales and eventually to South Australia. Stephen Hicks - a farmer in the North Cornish parish of St Mabyn - decided to migrate after reading an article on South Australia in *The Chambers Journal*. Richard Best, the son of an impoverished labourer, was advised to secure a passage to the colony by Parson Childs, the then Vicar of St Dennis.

Others were attached by affinity with South Australia's 'liberal, dissenting' atmosphere and by the feelings of freedom and opportunity which existed in the colony. Although the Cornish overseas retained a deep loyalty to Cornwall, they nevertheless looked back with a certain bitterness to the social system and deprivation they had left behind. Thomas Sleep, in a letter to his uncle in Falmouth, wrote that '. . . none of us wants to return to the bondage which holds our fellow-countrymen . . .' in Cornwall; and John Oats, a miner at Kapunda, urged his relatives to come out for their own 'welfare.' Indeed, glowing letters written home by Cornish settlers prompted further migration to South Australia. *The South Australian Register* was certainly correct when it observed that '. . . enough has transpired through the press or the private communications of those who have candidly sent home their favourable impressions to arouse the attention of the enterprising Cornish of all classes, from one end of the county to the other . . .'.

Charles Dunn wrote home to Lewannick in East Cornwall to persuade his friends Thomas Hawke and Thomas Buller to come out, and Thomas Scown informed his brother in the Cornish border town of Launceston that Cornish mechanics could be certain of employment, for 'We have not only given general satisfaction, but other mechanics are surprised at these Cornish operatives. Londoners, in South Australia, are already put by by Cornish men'.

More cautiously, S. Bray wrote to his relatives in Falmouth that 'I would not persuade anyone to leave their native land; but all steady men are sure to do much better for themselves in this country than at home'.

William Prowse, from Penzance, had no hesitations but was wildly enthusiastic and wanted to be joined in South Australia by all his friends and relatives: '. . . tell Uncle Richard of Crankan and all his family to come out and not delay no time, tell Uncle John Prowse to sell his house and come out and all his family, and James Marks and my sister likewise. We would wish if John and Nancy would come out here and Henry Nancervis, and all the rest if they can make up their mind . . . tell Aunt Alice to come out and not be afraid of the sea, and mother likewise'.

The general interest which had been created in Cornwall in the fortunes of the new colony was reinforced by South Australia's first mineral discoveries of galena, or silver-lead, at Glen Osmond in 1841. Soon articles were appearing in Cornish journals enthusing over the colony's mineral developments, and Cornish miners were attracted to the colony by the growing demand for skilled labour.

The Burra Burra Copper Mine, discovered in 1845, emerged as the principal employer of Cornishmen in the period to 1860. There developed a close relationship between the South Australian Mining Association (which ran the Burra Burra mine) and J. B. Wilcocks - a senior migration agent stationed in Plymouth, Devonshire. He had begun selecting Cornish miners for the Burra Burra in the mid-1840s, but was most especially useful to the S.A.M.A. during the Victorian gold rushes when many of the Burra Burra miners were lured away to the neighbouring colony in search of the yellow metal. In 1854, for example, Henry Ayers (the S.A.M.A. Secretary) wrote to Wilcocks offering him a bounty of £2 per head for up to five hundred Cornish miners. Not surprisingly, Wilcocks rose to the occasion, sending out a whole stream of Cousin Jacks at the earliest opportunity!

By 1849 the Burra Burra Mine had become established as a major copper producer and was contributing to the decline of the Cornish mining economy at home at a time when copper mines there were becoming very deep, less rich, and therefore more costly to work. It was a vicious circle, in fact. As the South Australian industry expanded, it further eroded the Cornish economy which sparked off still greater migration to the colony. A brief respite was provided for Cornwall by the Victorian gold rushes, when the Burra Burra and other mines had to suspend operations. But the vicious circle was again perpetuated by the discovery and exploitation of the wonderfully rich copper deposits at Wallaroo and Moonta in the early 1860s, in an area destined to become known as 'Australia's Little Cornwall'.

The expansion of the Wallaroo and Moonta Mines was facilitated at first by Cornish miners leaving the Burra Burra and the Victorian diggings, but soon they were joined by hundreds of other Cousin Jacks from Cornwall itself. Their migration was aided by the Sutherland Act of 1863 which reserved one-third of the annual land revenue to finance assisted immigration. In 1864, of all migrants over twenty per cent were from Cornwall, the small mining district of Marazion sending as many as 150 miners. And in 1865, a staggering forty-three per cent of persons entering the colony were of Cornish origin.

The great crash in Cornish copper occurred in 1866, when many of the famous and long-established Cornish mines were forced to close. Although a restrictive immigration policy from 1867 to 1871 served to prevent a flood of Cornishmen into South Australia, some 7830 miners left Cornwall for overseas during 1867. The 'Cornwall Central Relief Committee', too, still gave financial aid to migrants who could not secure assisted passages. Inevitably, many of these Cousin Jacks found their way to W allaroo and Moonta; and when a more liberal immigration scheme was introduced in 1872, Cornish families again migrated to South Australia in considerable numbers. Indeed, the *West Briton* newspaper noted that during 1875 no fewer than 10 567 migrants left Cornwall for the Australian colonies.

During the 1880s and 1890s depressed conditions in South Australian mining did not encourage Cornish migration to the colony, and Cousin Jacks were instead attracted to the gold and diamond fields of southern Africa. But one memorable occasion was the journey of Captain Richard Piper to Cornwall in 1883 to secure new recruits for the Wallaroo Mines. Piper inserted an advertisement in the *West Briton* which read 'Wanted immediately, Fifty good Miners, including steady young men, also married men with their families, to proceed to the Wallaroo Copper Mines, South Australia. For rates of wages and all particulars apply at once in person to Mr Richard Piper, 3 Falmouth-road, Redruth'.

Piper returned to South Australia on the *Oriana* with some 405 men, women, and children. These people settled at Wallaroo Mines in the special 'New Chums' cottages which had been built in anticipation of their arrival. Although they themselves probably did not realise it at the time, their migration constituted what was to be the last collective, large-scale movement of population from Cornwall to South Australia.

Once in South Australia, the Cornish were quick to assume a central role in the development of the colony's mining industry. Although the Cornish were rarely directors or shareholders in mining companies - a disconcerting fact for some Cousin Jacks who complained that South Australian capitalists were more concerned to profit through share speculation than to engage in serious investment - their influence ran deep in the economic organisation and practices of South Australian mining. The Cornish employment system of 'tribute' and 'tutwork' (that is, a system of individual contract between the miner and the employer, valid for a certain piece of work over a certain period of time) prevailed in almost all of the mines. On-site management was provided by 'grass' (surface) and 'underground' Cornish 'captains'.

Mining terminology was Cornish-inspired, so that clay-slate was always refered to as 'killas', a shaft bucket was a 'kibble', an exploratory trench a 'costeen', a good vein of ore a 'champion lode', a winding device a 'whim', and so on. Engine-houses - the buildings which housed the steam engines for winding, pumping, and ore-stamping - were built by Cornish masons to the classic Cornish designs. The actual engines they housed were constructed by Cornish foundries - at first in Cornwall by firms such as the Perran Foundry and Harvey & Co of Hayle, and later by Cornish-owned establishments in South

Australia which emerged to meet the needs of both mining and agriculture. Perhaps the most famous of these was Martin's of Gawler. From small beginnings in 1848, James Martin developed his foundry to the point where, at his death in 1899, it was employing 700 men and covered more than seven hectares of land. Other Cornish foundries included Hawke's of Kapunda, Rowe's of Strathalbyn, May's of Wallaroo, May Bros. of Gawler, Jones's of Adelaide, and Coumbe's of Kilkenny.

It can be hardly overstating the case to claim that wherever there was a mine in South Australia there was also a Cornishman. One would find the tell-tale Cornish names everywhere. Most people, perhaps, know that the Burra townships of Redruth and Copperhouse are named after Cornish centres (although the suburb of Lostwithiel is less well known), but few know that Truro is 'named after the Cornish glory'. Even fewer will have heard of the Cornish named settlements of Penrice, near Angaston; Helston, near Kapunda; or Saltash in the north of the State near the New South Wales border.

In the late 1850s, one South Australian newspaper dubbed the Mount Barker mining district 'the Cornwall of Australia' - and no wonder, with the Cornish-named villages of Callington, Kelynack and St Ives and a whole string of mines echoing the names of Old Cornwall. Indeed, a great many South Australian mine names betrayed Cornish origins. Over fifty mines bore the Cornish prefix 'wheal' (literally, 'a working'), and they read like a roll call from Cornwall itself - Wheal Virgin, Wheal Basset, Wheal Rose, Wheal Prosper, Wheal Grenfell, Wheal Friendship and so on. They were to be found all over the colony and in every conceivable geographic location - Wheal Mary at Normanville, Wheal Gleeson at Yudnamutana, Wheal Hancock north-east of Beltana, Great Wheal Orford at Tungkillo, Wheal Sarah at Clare...

Other mine names revealed Cornish affiliations, too, such as Trevue, New Cornwall, Truro, Duke of Cornwall, while still others took the names of mines back home - Tresevean (sic), Carn Brea, Botallick (sic), Dalcooth (sic), Crinnis - perhaps in the hope that in time they would come to equal or surpass their Cornish namesakes. On the smaller workings, individual Cornishmen sometimes gave their own names to the mines. Thus we find Benalack Mine, Jago and Harris' Prospect at Uroonda, Paull's Consolidated and Paull's North Extended at Mount Lyndhurst, Davey's Mine, Trenowden's Claim at Trinity Dam, Hooper's Luck, Jenkin's Claim, Hicks' Shaft on Kangaroo Island, Vickery's Claim, Kirkeek's Treasure, and so on.

For the most part, South Australian mines were managed by Cornishmen. J. A. Tregoning was secretary of Wheal Barton at Truro whilst Captain Peters was the mine's manager. Captain Martin was at Yudnamutana, Messrs Alfred Jenkin & Son ran the Talisker Mine at Cape Jervis, and Captain Tonkin spent some time at the Kanyaka Mine ninety-three kilometres from Port Augusta. Captain Doble, formerly a manager in Cornwall and in Spain, was at Blinman - as were Captains Anthony and Bryant - and. Captain Pascoe was at the Glen Osmond Mines.

Captain George Vercoe opened up various mines on the Eyre Peninsula, whilst Captain Richard Rodda was involved with several enterprises in the Angaston district. Captains Trestrail and Penrose developed the Boolcoomatta claim, 220 kilometres north-east of the Burra Burra. Captain Cock, quite appropriately, was engaged to work the Bird-in-Hand mine at Woodside; and the Nuccaleena Mine in the Flinders Ranges was run by Captain Pearson Morrison, 'a gentleman of considerable experience both in America and Cornwall'. For a time, Captain Doney was at Kanmantoo, and Captain Prisk was a manager at the various Strathalbyn mines. Captain Tregoweth was manager of the small Parara Mine at Ardrossan on mid-Yorke Peninsula in 1874, but soon moved on to several other workings, ultimately to run the Mutooroo mine near Cockburn on the New South Wales border.

However, despite this widespread influence, by far the greatest concentration of Cornish captains, and indeed of Cornish miners, was in the 'copper triangle' of northern Yorke Peninsula - the localities of Moonta, Wallaroo and Kadina which together earned the collective title of 'Australia's Little Cornwall'. The presence of copper in the area had been noted as early as the 1840s, but the first major find was on the Wallaroo run - a pastoral property - in 1859. A party of Cornish miners was brought over to Wallaroo from the Burra, and mining operations commenced. By the middle of 1860 some 150 miners were employed at the Wallaroo Mines, while the principal shaft was already down twelve fathoms (twelve-two metres).

During 1861 the neighbouring Moonta Mines were discovered and soon numerous other mineral claims were being worked in the area - the Wandilta, the Goldsworthy, the New Cornwall, the Karkarilla, the Yelta, the Doora, and many others. Thus although the Wallaroo and Moonta mines came to dominate South Australian mining, they were by no means the only ventures in northern Yorke Peninsula. The *Yorke's Peninsula Advertiser* in May 1873 noted the names, captains and secretaries of no fewer than fifty-four separate mines. A number of these were never much more than small pits in the ground, whilst others were soon incorporated into the two large companies. But others, such as the Hamley and the Yelta, retained their independence long after the disappearance of the smaller and more obscure workings.

Cornish miners, who had previously laboured at Burra or Kapunda, in the Adelaide Hills or the Flinders Ranges, at Ballarat or Bendigo, or indeed in Camborne or Callington, were drawn to 'Little Cornwall' as the mines increased in size and importance. The Moonta Mines soon became established as the richest concern in the locality, and in their first year of operation they realised a profit of £101,000 from 9000 tonnes of ore raised. This prosperity continued until the late 1870s, when increasing costs and low copper prices caused the company to sustain two years of loss. Profitability was restored through good management and as a result of more favourable economic conditions, but by 1888 the Moonta Mines were again in trouble.

The Wallaroo Mines had not proved as spectacularly rich as their Moonta counterparts, but nevertheless were profitable until the late 1870s when hard times were encountered. The mines were then worked intermittently for several years and, although full-scale production was restored in the early 1880s, they were never, in the rest of their independent life, as great as in the former period. Indeed, by 1888 the company's financial position was again parlous.

The common problems of the Moonta and Wallaroo mines in the late 1880s led the directors of both companies to decide that amalgamation was necessary. Combined operations would afford various economies of scale, whilst a large firm would be more able to withstand the pressures of adverse economic conditions. Thus a merger was effected in 1890, forming the extensive Wallaroo and Moonta Mining and Smelting Company.

This amalgamation injected a new lease of life into the northern Yorke Peninsula mining district, so that in the period to 1923 as much copper was produced as in the decades before the merger. The combined company was the largest industrial concern in South Australia. It completely outlived the entire Cornish copper industry whilst faring at least as well as Cornish tin. The Wallaroo Mines, in particular, received considerable modernisation and capital investment; there was a marked transfer of labour and materials to Wallaroo Mines from Moonta Mines. Production from the underground workings of the latter declined after 1890, and greater attention was focused on the re-treatment of wastes through the cementation process.

The first World War, although causing initial dislocation in the industry, increased the demand for copper, and so from 1915 to 1918 both mines were working at full capacity. With the end of the war, however, came a sharp fall in the price of copper - a fall from which the mines never recovered. The company survived as a marginal concern from 1919 until 1923, but by then closure was inevitable. And so, almost unbelievably, the pump engines were stopped completely for the first time in nearly sixty years, the miners made redundant, and the mining plant dismantled. At last Wallaroo and Moonta were at one with the 'knacked bals' of Cornwall. The abandoned wastes of northern Yorke Peninsula soon came to acquire the same desolate, haunting atmosphere which one senses so strongly in Gwennap, on Caradon Hill, or in any of the other old Cornish mining districts.

But despite the ultimate demise of the locality as a copper-producing area, it must be remembered that the mines' longevity was something of a record in the annals of South Australian mining. The development, prosperity and survival of the Wallaroo and Moonta mines is to be attributed, to a very great degree, to the exceptional management of Henry Richard Hancock and his son, H. Lipson Hancock.

Captain H. R. Hancock began his mining career at the mighty Cornish copper mine of Devon Great Consols, on the Devonshire bank of the Tamar. He came to South Australia in his early twenties to work at Wheal Ellen, near Strathalbyn. From there he moved to the Yelta mine and in 1864, on the dismissal of the unsatisfactory Captain Warmington, became principal Captain of the Moonta Mines. He was also Captain of Wallaroo Mines for some time during their independent existence, and in 1890 became Manager of the amalgamated company.

In contrast with the poor development and lack of scientific treatment at the Burra Burra Mine, the expansion of the Moonta Mines was characterised by prudent ore conservation, technical innovation, and sensible planning. This was in no small measure the result of the policies of H. R. Hancock. He dominated the mines (and mining settlements) with a rule of benevolent dictatorship. He was responsible for numerous improvements at Moonta, such as the introduction of man skips (which enabled the miners to ride to surface, instead of having to climb up endless fathoms of ladders) and the use of large-than-standard kibbles (which facilitated the removal of large amounts of ore). He was also the inventor of the celebrated 'Hancock Jig', used in the processing of the ores, and developed his own design of pneumatic drill for use underground at the mines. Captain Hancock's son studied mining engineering at Ballarat and was one of a new breed of Australian mine managers. He succeeded his father in 1898 and was responsible for the widespread modernisation of the mines. He opposed the use of the title Captain (but was unsuccessful in trying to eradicate it) and did much to transform Wallaroo and Moonta from typical nineteenth-century Cornish mines to modern industrial units. But despite his love of progress and order, he was, although born in Australia, cast very much in the Cornish mould. He spoke with a marked Cornish accent, and one of his contemporaries recalled that 'Lipson Hancock had all the Cornish virtues and only one of the vices. He was warm-hearted, hospitable, and genuinely concerned for the welfare of those under him. On Sunday afternoon he visited any old miner who was seriously ill. Lipson's one limitation - and he knew it - was that of suspiciousness, characteristic of Cornishmen'.

The mining settlements which grew up in association with the mines of 'Little Cornwall' were all curiously individualistic, each with its own identity and atmosphere. Government townships were laid out at Kadina and Moonta, in the heart of the mining district, and with their symmetry and rectangular design were typical of country towns all over South Australia. A township was also founded at Port Wallaroo, on the coast some distance west of the mines, where a jetty and smelting works were constructed. These three towns became the commercial centres of the district, supporting a mixed population of Cornish settlers and artisans of English, Scots, Irish or German descent. Port Wallaroo, or just Wallaroo as it came to be known, also sported a strong Welsh element, because of the smelting works being situated there. One ex-resident recalled that the town's inhabitants were 'mostly from Wales and Cornwall'.

In addition to the three townships, there were a variety of off-shoots and suburbs. Menadue and Jericho were names reminiscent of Cornwall, whilst others - Cross Roads, Yelta, East Moonta - indicated their geographical positions. But the most sizeable off-shoots were Moonta Mines and Wallaroo Mines; the latter, confusingly, being situated some kilometres from Wallaroo township and being in reality a westward extension of Kadina. Both the 'Mines' settlements were overwhelmingly Cornish, consisting of miners' cottages built in an *ad hoc* fashion on the actual mineral leases. The miners themselves built their cottages, utilising local materials, and enlarged them as the settlements became more permanent or as families grew. They presented a strange spectacle to the visitor and seemed dotted without reason or order among the mine-buildings, shaft-openings, and waste-heaps.

Life in the settlements was rarely easy. Yorke Peninsula is practically devoid of natural water deposits. In drought years 'Little Cornwall' was faced with severe water shortages. Tanks sunk into the ground to collect rain water were only a partial solution to the problem, and when they became stagnant promoted disease. Typhoid and other forms of fever swept the district from time to time, causing widespread illness and decimating the infant population.

Nevertheless, life went on, and the social and cultural environment the miners created bore all the marks of a strong Cornish influence. Physically, the mining area, with its massive Cornish engine houses dominating the scene, was strikingly reminiscent of Cornwall. The patterns of working-life were the same as at home, particularly as miners often worked alongside friends and relatives who had been formerly their colleagues in the Cornish mines. And for the newly-arrived miner, it was comforting to find familiar faces and customs in this 'Little Cornwall' on the other side of the world. One Cousin Jack described the misgivings he felt as he approached Kadina for the first time and then went on: 'But just as the coach pulled up, someone called out, "Who's that - old Bill? - how is Redruth looking?", meaning the place I came from in Cornwall, and then another called out, "Is there anyone there from Camborne?" Thus was my reception at Kadina. As I soon found out, I was not the only one from Cornwall, and I replied asking, "How is the bal looking?", meaning the mine, and the answer was, "Plenty of ore!"'

When the Cornish Association of South Australia was formed in 1890, a strong branch was established in 'Little Cornwall' (there were other branches in Clare, Gawler, and Adelaide, together with a similar association at Broken Hill). And it was not only the men folk who experienced sentiments of Cornish fellowship: Thomas Cowling recalled that at Yelta, 'all the women were natives of Cornwall, and so a spirit of comradeship grew up among them'. Anthony Trollope, the novelist, visited the area in the early 1870s and wrote that 'so many of the miners were Cornishmen as to give Moonta and Wallaroo the air of Cornish towns'. Nearly forty years later, May Vivienne, in her *Sunny South Australia*, could still write that 'the majority of the miners in the district are Cornishmen' and note that the local shops 'do a big trade in Cornish pasties'. Similarly, in 1909, W. G. Spence could reflect on the district, observing that the people 'lived isolated from the rest of the colony, remaining more Cornish than Cornwall itself'.

Indeed, this isolation was important in maintaining 'Little Cornwall's' sense of difference, for the peninsula was cut off from the main body of South Australia and was certainly remote from other principal centres of population in the colony. As in Cornwall, people from outside were labelled foreigners, and one Adelaide man who sought employment in the district remembered sourly that his 'first impression of Moonta Mines was - what had I let myself in for? It was soon made clear that I was a foreigner, with habits and opinions to be viewed with suspicion.'

The Cornish settlers in 'Little Cornwall' were aware of their individuality, too, and some spoke openly of the district as 'our Cornish colony'. On formal occasions, such as the writing of a letter or the completion of an official form, they would describe their country of birth as England. But, unofficially, their sentiments were rather different as evidenced by the old man who wrote to the *Kadina and Wallaroo Times* recalling the days when he was 'a boay 'ome to Cornwall, near England'.

Similarly, in 1867, when it was rumoured that operations at the Moonta Mines might be suspended, a mass meeting of miners was held to discuss the situation. Just as political leaders in South Australia would later evoke the Cornish motto 'One and All', so the miners responded to the threat of closure with a resolution declaring, 'Here's five thousand Cornishmen will know the reason why' - a direct allusion to the old Cornish jingle (formalised into a ballad by the Reverend R. S. Hawker) which had grown into a kind of Cornish national anthem:

And Shall Trelawney Die?
Here's Twenty-thousand Cornishmen
Will know the Reason Why!

Not surprisingly, the Cornish accent and dialect persisted in 'Little Cornwall' for many years. Indeed, it is still possible to discern something of the Cornish vowel sounds, lilt, and word order in the speech of the more elderly people at Moonta Mines. Stanley Whitford, the Moonta-born Labor politician, freely admitted that he spoke with a distinct Cornish accent, and he said of other Cousin Jacks born on the Peninsula, 'You would think they came direct from Cornwall when you listened to their Cornish brogue'. Likewise, in 1907, the *Australian Christian Commonwealth* could note in an obituary of one Benjamin Rose that, 'he was a native-born Australian, but coming of Cornish parents and having spent so many years in that Cornwall beneath the Southern Cross, Moonta, his speech betrayed his descent'.

Surnames, too, betrayed the origins of the Peninsula folk, many of them the proud inheritors of old Cornish Celtic and patronymic names, such as Davey, Penalurick, Phillips, Blight, Scown, Blewett, Mitchell, Goldsworthy, Kemp, Dunstan, Daddow, Sandow, Thomas, Verran, Hosking, Kinsman, Bice, Deeble, Hawke, Lanyon, Kitto, Bray, Wearne, Osborne, Williams, Trenwith, Vercoe, Cock, Jago, Prisk, Penhall, Knuckey, Rodda, Cowling, Waters, Pollard, Rowe, Richards, Mutton, Skews, Craddock, Moyle, Tonkin, Roberts, Champion, Johns, Martin, Kessell, Trezise, Trevivian, Besanko, Nankeville, Warren, Pengelly, Nicholls, Polkinghorne, Pryor, Tamblyn, Dawe, Opie, Rosewarne, and countless others.

Cornish customs, sayings, and superstitions were maintained. There were plenty of mining proverbs such as 'mundic rides a good horse' (that is, arsenic and pyritic rock suggests the presence of payable lodes), and 'Jack o' Lanterns' (members of the faery brethren) were said to move across the paddocks at night, indicating the positions of ore bodies. On the strength of one such sighting in 1863, a company was formed to work the ground over which the Jack o' Lantern had moved. And as late as 1921, Captain W. H. Hayes, in a technical report compiled for H. Lipson Hancock, discussed seriously the supernatural powers of local residents who claimed to be ore diviners.

Naughty children at Moonta, Wallaroo and Kadina, many of whom had never set foot on Cornish soil, would be chastised with the threat that they would be 'took to Bodmin' (Bodmin Gaol in Cornwall), and a new-born babe would have his gums rubbed with brandy - supposedly a legacy of Cornwall's smuggling days - to ensure that he would never die by hanging. Housewives in 'Little Cornwall' continued to prepare traditional

Cornish foods, such as pasties, saffron cake, 'heavy' cake, and jam and cream 'splits'. Home brewing was popular, as it was in Cornwall, and the Peninsula miners developed their own brand of beer called Swanky.

For the working-class Cornish, entertainment was provided by Cornish wrestling bouts which were held not only in 'Little Cornwall', but in other areas of South Australia where there were concentrations of Cornish folk. In the 1840s great matches, billed as Cornwall versus Devonshire, were staged in King William Street, Adelaide; and Cornish wrestling was important in the early mining days at the Burra. It could still draw large crowds at the end of the century at Broken Hill when many of South Australia's Cousin Jacks went to the Barrier silver-lead fields in search of work.

On northern York Peninsula, Corriish wrestling matches were held traditionally over Easter and at Christmas, although additional bouts were often held at other times in the year. The popular venues were Moyle's Hotel at Wallaroo and Nankervis's Hotel at Kadina. The matches were impressive affairs, the contestants being 'some of the best wrestlers out of Cornwall'. One memorable clash was that between the Moonta champion and the Ballarat champion in 1868. Watched by a record crowd, they struggled for hours with equal points until suddenly the Moonta champion, 'Dancing Bray', floored his opponent with a superbly executed Flying Mare trick - a wrestling throw still recognised in Cornwall today.

Another manifestation of Cornish culture in 'Little Cornwall' were the midsummer bonfires, actually held in midwinter to correspond with midsummer's eve in Cornwall and to avoid the danger of causing bushfires. Numerous bonfires were lit in the settlements - on waste ground and in backyards - and were attended by hundreds of people who sang songs, let off fireworks, and roasted potatoes in their jackets in the dying embers of the fires as the evening drew to a close. Some of the more exuberant miners also set off explosive charges they had 'borrowed' from the magazine, with spectacular but unnerving effect. This was perhaps a survival of the old Cornish miners' custom of 'shooting' (blasting) holes in rock formations to celebrate the coming of midsummer.

Just as fierce rivalries had grown up between neighbouring townships in Cornwall - between Camborne and Redruth, Gorran and Mevagissey, Padstow and Wadebridge - so a spirit of intense competition developed between the various settlements of 'Little Cornwall'. To the Moonta Mines folk, people from East Moonta were 'copper tails', while those from Moonta township were nicknamed 'silver tails' - a distinction reflecting the supposed social superiority of the townspeople over the mineral-lease dwellers, a kind of inverted snobbery. Fighting between gangs of youths from the different settlements was not unknown, and local societies were fraught with divisions as a result of the mutual mistrust and suspicion which existed between the areas. The Yorke Peninsula Football Association, for example, was formed on 20 March 1888 from teams in the locality. But as early as 4 May of that year a serious dispute had broken out between Moonta Mines Young Turks and Wallaroo, resulting in the resignation of an umpire and a replay on neutral ground at Kadina - an occurence which set the tone for future relationships between the teams.

The Cornish generally, with their strong nonconformist background, were suspicious of Irish-Catholic elements in the community, although the fierce inter-Celtic rivalry which flared from time to time at Kapunda was never matched on Yorke Peninsula due to the relatively small size of the Irish population there. Nevertheless, this did not prevent the Cornish from forming a vigorous Orange Lodge, nor did it dampen the enthusiasm of the various Methodist denominations which were active in the area.

The Bible Christians (a denomination with its roots firmly embedded in Cornwall), the Primitive Methodists, and the Wesleyans were all well represented in 'Little Cornwall'. A Bible Christian chapel had been opened in the area as early as 1861, and by 1875 there were no fewer than fourteen chapels in and around Moonta, with over twenty chapels within the 'copper triangle' of Wallaroo, Moonta, and Kadina. Many South Australian Methodist ministers were themselves Cornishmen, and in addition there were countless local preachers, class leaders, and Sunday School superintendents who hailed from west of the Tamar. In the 1880s, with the growth of farming on Yorke Peninsula, chapels also sprang up in the outlying districts, while 'Methodism at Maitland was pioneered from Wallaroo, Moonta and Kadina'.

The Methodist influence was important in moulding many facets of Cornish culture, not least the musical aspects of both worship and entertainment. The Cornish were - like their cousins, the Welsh - great lovers of singing. Cornish Carols flourished at Moonta and Kadina with local musicians such as 'Fiddler Jim' Richards and Johnnie Thomas adding to the traditional Cornish repertoire. Other local composers to emerge included Edward Quintrell, Joseph Glasson, William Holman, and Leslie Davey and in 1893 a compendium of local hymns was published under the title *The Christmas Welcome: A Choice Collection of Cornish Carols*.

'Banding' was the Cornishman's other great musical pastime. Innumerable brass, fife and drum, and other bands existed; some, like the ubiquitous Bargwanna's Band, seemed to turn out at the slightest excuse to lead the parades of the Amalgamated Miners' Association, the Rechabite Lodge, the Orange Order, the Methodist Sunday Schools, and the various other religious and temperance organisations in the district. But perhaps the most famous of them all was the Wallaroo Brass Band, founded in 1895 - the forerunner of today's Kadina and Wallaroo Brass Band.

The Methodist influence, too, was felt in political life. The nonconformist-radical tradition which developed in Cornwall found a mirror image on Yorke Peninsula where Methodist local preachers such as Reuben Gill - known as 'The Billy Bray of South Australia' after the famous Cornish preacher - were also trade union activists and foundation members of the United Labor Party. Although industrial unrest was never as marked at Moonta and Wallaroo as it was at Broken Hill, there were a number of significant strikes between 1864 and 1921, with the Wallaroo constituency emerging as a major U.L.P. stronghold. Cornish-born Richard Hooper was the first Labor M.P. for the district - and the first Labor member of the House of Assembly. In later years 'Little Cornwall' gave South Australia two Labor Premiers: John Verran (from 1910 to 1912) and R. S. Richards (1933). Both were of typical Cornish mining backgrounds - the former born in Gwennap, Cornwall, the latter at Moonta Mines, and both were local preachers in the Methodist Church.

With the closure of the Moonta and Wallaroo Mines in 1923, it was inevitable that the Cornish atmosphere of the locality would become less pronounced. Families moved away, to the mines at Broken Hill, to the smelting town of Port Pirie, to Adelaide, Whyalla, and other centres. For those who remained, the Cornish background became less relevant as the years passed, particularly for the generations born on South Australian soil for whom Cornwall was just a name in family lore. Certain traditions, such as Cornish wrestling and midsummer bonfires, had disappeared even before the mine closures; although other features of the Cornish inheritance, such as chapel life and banding, survived and even flourished.

Today, the Cornish influence in 'Little Cornwall' is essentially a historical, retrospective thing, although some of the more elderly people in the remaining cottages on the Mines settlements live in a manner not much changed from the 1920s and 1930s. Others have joined the Cornish Association of South Australia in a conscious act of preserving Cornish links. The cartoons and writings of the late Oswald Pryor, produced over a long period from 1900 to the mid-1960s, did much to focus attention on the district's Cornish heritage, as did the novel *Not Only In Stone* by Phyllis Somerville.

The 'Back to Moonta' festival in 1927 was an opportunity for the town to remember its Cornish origins. The various jubilees, copper centenaries and local government centenaries have also proved opportunities to recall the pioneering efforts of Cousin Jack. The Moonta, Wallaroo and Kadina branches of the National Trust of South Australia work hard to preserve and promote the local history, but today the greatest expression of the area's Cornish past is the magnificent Kernewek Lowender Cornish Festival. First staged in 1973, this biennial festival has become increasingly successful, indeed so much so that interest in 'Australia's Little Cornwall' has been rekindled - not only in South Australia but all over Australia and in Cornwall itself.

Prelude

The creation of 'Little Cornwall' at Moonta, Wallaroo and Kadina in the decades after 1860 was the pinnacle of Cornish achievement in South Australia, and indeed in Australia as a whole. Yet the Cousin Jacks had made a vital and lasting impression on South Australian development even before the first mineral discoveries on northern Yorke Peninsula. The mines at Glen Osmond, Kapunda and Montacute were opened up with the help of Cornish miners, but two mining districts in particular became associated with the Cousin Jacks - Burra Burra, and the tract of mineralised country running through Mount Barker to Callington. Discovered in 1845, the Burra Burra Mine at its height was one of the largest copper mines in the world, and it was worked (though not continuously) until 1877. The Mount Barker group was worked sporadically throughout the last century, the principal mines being the Preamimma, the Kanmantoo, the Paringa, the Bremer, the Aclare, the Menkoo, the Tresevean, Wheal Friendship, Wheal Margaret, and Wheal Fortune. In a sense, therefore, the Burra and Mount Barker districts were the 'Little Cornwalls' of South Australia's first mining era - a fact noted by contemporary observers. As such they were a kind of prelude to the later era at Moonta, Wallaroo and Kadina.

Left, top: A classic view of the Callington (or Bremer) Mine. It would be difficult, even in Cornwall, to find a more perfect example of a nineteenth-century Cornish mine. The engine houses - white-washed, as was the Cornish practice in the earlier days - are of typical Cornish design, the one on the left housing a pump engine and the one on the right housing a whim (or winding engine). In the centre is a horse whim, complete with horse. Note, too, the narrow, Cornish wheelbarrows that were in use. The Callington Mine was first discovered in 1849, and in its earlier years attracted considerable interest on account of its successful use of the Vyan rake buddle in minimising the percentage of copper discarded with the wastes. A small smelting works was erected at the mine by the Thomas brothers from Hayle, in Cornwall. Numerous Cousin Jacks found employment in the Callington and Kanmantoo area - men like Thomas Nicholls from St Austell, John Orchard from Wendron, and Absalom Tonkin from St Blazey.

Left: Part of the Burra Burra Mine workings as they appeared in 1874, in their declining years. Features of interest include the crushing plant and waterwheel on the extreme left; the complex launder construction conveying water to the wheel; Peacock's pump house, chimney and whim in the centre background; and Shneider's stack on the hill at the far right of the picture. The mine was managed from 1847 until 1868 by Captain Henry Roach who hailed from Redruth, Cornwall. He worked for some time at the Tresavean mine, where his uncle was a Captain, before leaving Cornwall to journey to South America and finally to Australia. Another Burra Burra notable was Captain Isaac Killicoat, who arrived in the colony in May 1853 to manage the Patent Copper Company's smelting works at the Burra Burra. He was born in the Cornish village of Perranwell in 1809, and was also employed at the Tresavean mine as a 'Grass' Captain before Coming to South Australia.

The Wallaroo Mines

With Moonta's claim to be 'the hub of the universe', it is often forgotten that the Wallaroo Mines were in fact discovered in 1859, while the neighbouring Moonta copper lodes were not located until 1861. Although in the period to 1889 the Moonta Mines outshone their Wallaroo counterparts in terms of fame and riches, the years after the amalgamation of the two companies witnessed a resurgence at the Wallaroo Mines manifested in widespread modernisation and capital investment. The photographs in this section clearly show the transition which occurred at Wallaroo Mines between 1890 and 1910. Gradually the stone-built engine houses, with their ponderous Cornish beam engines, were demolished and replaced by more modern mining plant; and the flimsy poppet heads or 'shears' gave way to the gigantic head frames which became characteristic of the Wallaroo Mines in the twentieth century. The modernisation process was accelerated by the disastrous fire at Taylor's Shaft in 1904. There, the engine and its pit work were damaged beyond repair, and there were serious runs of ground due to the destruction of underground timbering. As a result, the upper part of the shaft and workings were permanently sealed off, and a new shaft was sunk from the surface to connect with the lower levels. At the same time, new electric pumps were installed underground to replace the wrecked Cornish engine.

Left: Elder's pump engine as it appeared soon after its installation at Wallaroo Mines in 1887. The engine was originally constructed by Harvey and Co. of Hayle, Cornwall, for the New Cornwall Mine at Kadina at a reputed cost of £30,000. It was later sold to Wallaroo Mines at £3000 and, curiously, the engine house was included in the sale. Each stone was numbered, then the building dismantled and re-erected at Wallaroo Mines. The engine was worked right up to the mine's closure in 1923, when the engine house was again dismantled and the stones used to construct the local Roman Catholic Church. The engine was on an enormous scale, the cylinder measuring 80 in. (2 metre) in diameter and the beam or 'bob' weighing all of 30 tonnes. The engine had a 13-ft. (4-metre) stroke, working at an average of 5 strokes per minute. Moulded into the bob was the legend 'New Cornwall Mines, South Australia, F. W. Bassett Engineer, 1862'.

Above: A group of mine workers at Wallaroo Mines around the turn of the century. The first three standing men from left to right are W. Bailey (engine driver), W. Polkinghorne, and R. Nicholls. The miner sitting in the centre left is J. Hancock. The wide-brimmed hat and neckerchief of the man standing on the extreme right seems to suggest the influence of the North American mining camps, where perhaps he had spent some time, while the underground outfits of the other miners are typically Cornish - especially the pressed-felt helmets to which tallow candles were fixed with lumps of clay in true Cornish style. In his right hand, Hancock is holding a 'crib bag' which no doubt contains his lunch-time pasty.

Right, top: A panoramic view of the mines looking east in 1890. On the extreme left are the buildings of the Devon Concentrating Plant, while in the right foreground is the Home whim engine - the first to be installed at Wallaroo Mines. In the centre background is Elder's pump engine, and in the distance the engine house of the neighbouring Matta Matta mine can just be discerned. This scene, strongly reminiscent of Cornwall, contrasts strikingly with following photographs depicting the Wallaroo Mines in the latter days of operation.

Right: The Wallaroo Mines blacksmiths, displaying a variety of calipers and hats.

WALLAROO MINES:- General view East from Office Shaft.

Top, left: The face of modern technology - Office Shaft sometime between 1900 to 1910. Situated from left to right are the ore-sorting plant (with hopper trucks standing alongside), head frame, weighbridge, and winding house. The 2-4-0T tank locomotive, constructed by Dubs and Co., was one of two originally used on the railway connecting the Adelaide seaside suburbs of Brighton and Glenelg.

Top, right: A group of Captains preparing to embark upon a tour of inspection of the underground workings in the early years of this century. Second from the left is H. Lipson Hancock, Superintendent of the amalgamated company from 1898 to 1923. The rather diminutive figure on the extreme right of the photograph is Thomas Tamblyn, 'the last of the old brigade', as Oswald Pryor termed him, a man who 'played bowls, umpired cricket matches, grew flowers, loved a good horse, and spoke in a rich Cornish dialect'. Also in the photograph is James Pryor. Born in 1845 at Rame in the West Cornish parish of Wendron, he worked from an early age in the local tin mines - Retanna Hill and the Wheal Lovell group - before coming to Ballarat in 1866 and Yorke Peninsula in 1869.

Above: The period of transition. A general view of Wallaroo Mines about 1903, illustrating the gradual replacement of obsolete equipment with modern plant. Traditional Cornish engine houses - either in use, as is Harvey's pump house in the background, or lying derelict, as is the partially demolished building on the left - rub shoulders with tall, steel chimney stacks and mighty head frames.

Top: The great fire at Taylor's Shaft, 1904. The fire was first noticed at three in the afternoon on 13 January and soon, as illustrated here, groups of anxious relatives congregated at the pit head, waiting for news of those trapped underground. As the flames were brought under control, parties of volunteers went below to rescue those overcome by the fumes and smoke. One miner later recalled the scene as the choking men were brought to surface: '. . . there must have been . . . from 150 to 200 men and they were all gassed, little or much. It was a pitiful sight to see those men brought up gassed, some of them being helpless, while others were dead to the world. As one after the other were brought to the surface, it was like bringing wounded men from a battlefield. And the strongest and largest men seemed to be the most affected. Some of them were brought up preaching and praying, others came up laughing, and some crying, and some very quiet'. Although none lost his life in the fire, many of the men were never the same again, a number apparently dying prematurely of various lung disorders caused or aggravated by the 'gas'.

Above: The new Taylor's Shaft at Wallaroo Mines, constructed after the disastrous fire of 1904. The company made a virtue out of necessity by integrating the reconstruction of the shaft and its plant into the general modernisation programme. From left to right are the ore storage bin, head frame, and winding house.

Left, top: A magnificent photograph of Office Shaft as it appeared in the period of 1900 to 1910. The stairways in the centre of the picture gave access to the ore storage bins, and to the ore sorting plant where a large number of pickey boys and old men worked at grading the ore.

Left: Aged men and pickey boys at Office Shaft in 1908. In 1871 it had been decided that no boys under the age of ten years were to be employed on the mines, except in the case of widow's sons who could be taken on when they reached nine. At both Wallaroo and Moonta, boys employed by the mines were expected to attend night school or day school at least three times a week, for a minimum of six hours in total. Old hands becoming too aged or inform to continue to work underground were often found jobs in the ore-sorting plant to enable them to continue earning money. This attitude to young boys and old men was indicative of the welfare policies developed at Wallaroo and Moonta - policies which reached their high point in the 'Betterment Principle' formulated by H. Lipson Hancock.

Above: The Wallaroo Mines mechanics in 1905 - again, an interesting array of implements and hats! Particularly noteworthy is the narrow Cornish-style wheelbarrow, evidence that they were still in general use at the mines well into this century.

Above: Young's Shaft in the 1900s. The crusher in the foreground and the head frame behind were erected to replace the old engine house and Cornish engine which had stood there in former days. The conical waste-tip in the background is of interest. Its shape is due to the method of dumping employed. A skip-way runs up one side of the tip to its apex, from where the skip deposits its load, thus perpetuating the conical shape. This method of tipping was also employed by the china clay industry in Cornwall, and largely accounted for the 'lunar landscape' which characterises the moors to the north of St Austell.

Left: A general view of Wallaroo Mines in 1905, looking west. The large white building with its tall stack is the power house, and to its right can be seen Home Shaft and a part of the mechanical shop yards. In the middle distance can be seen Office Shaft, with its large head frame and ore-sorting plant. To the right of Office Shaft is the count house and mine stores; and in the background - from left to right - are Young's Shaft, Harvey's attle-crushing plant, and Harvey's pump engine. In the top right-hand corner, are the miner's cottages which form the suburb of Jericho.

Settlements: Kadina and Wallaroo Mines

The settlement called Wallaroo Mines was originally, in 1860, a collection of tents and huts quickly put up by the first Cornish miners to give them temporary protection from the elements. Then, like Topsy, the settlement 'just growed' as more miners arrived and more dwellings were constructed. When it became clear that the mines were rich and likely to last, these houses were made more permanent.

Kadina, the adjourning township, was by contrast a more consciously-planned affair, and developed as a thriving country town. Its various shops and other commercial enterprises served the needs of the local mining community. People would walk into Kadina from Wallaroo Mines to do their shopping or to see to other business, for the two settlements were very closely connected, both physically and economically. The one was dependant upon the other.

Left, top: This photograph was taken some time between 1915 and 1921, and thus this cottage (from the evidence of its caption) was probably constructed between 1865 and 1870. It stood in Ewing Street, Kadina, and is interesting as it reveals something of the method of construction of these early cottages. The side wall is apparently a mixture of stone and wattle and daub, and the front is made from roughly hewn planks of wood. The two trees have been strategically planted to give shade from the fierce mid-summer sun.

Left: A view of Kadina looking north-west, around 1898 to 1903. Pavements, telegraph poles and substantial buildings attest to the town's size and importance. Also portrayed is the rambling, ribbon development which characterised the growth of the Yorke Peninsula mining districts and is reminiscent of the very similar ribbon development noticeable in Cornwall's Camborne-Redruth mining zone.

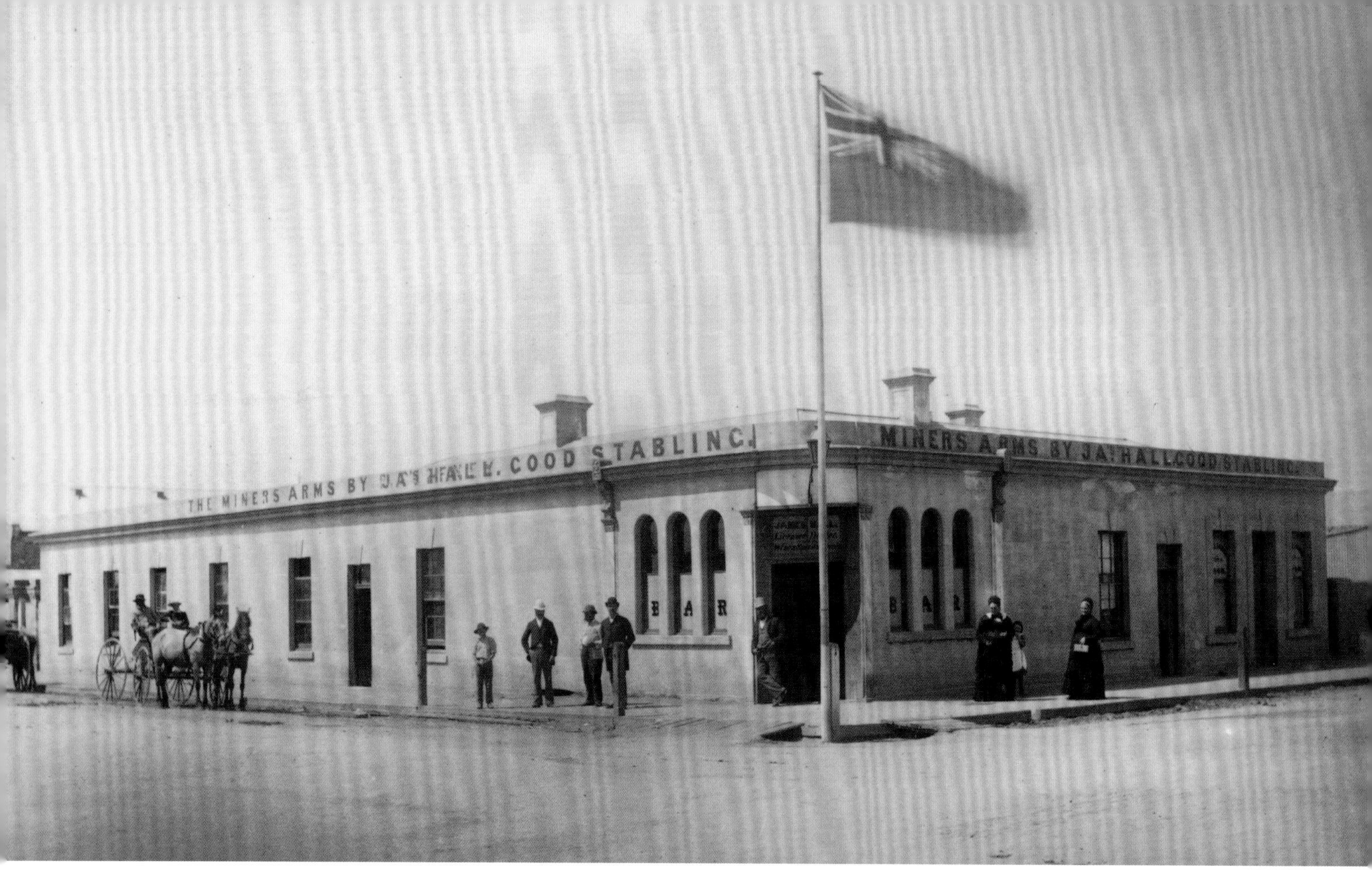

THE MINERS ARMS BY JA'S HALL. GOOD STABLING.
MINERS ARMS BY JA'S HALL GOOD STABLING
BAR
BAR

Left, top: James Hall's Miners Arms Hotel, Kadina, as it appeared between 1880 and 1890. Although the Cornish were often Methodists, and frequently members of temperance movements, drinking - and sometimes hard drinking - was certainly not unknown, either in Cornwall or on Yorke Peninsula. For many years there was a much-frequented 'kiddleywink' or sly-grog shop on a sandhill between the Karkarilla and Hamley mines at Moonta, together with a number of hotels in the three towns. Of course there was also the widespread home brewing of 'swanky'.

Left: The staff of John Henry Rosewarne's blacksmith and wheelwright business in Kadina, around 1886. J. H. Rosewarne was born at the Burra in 1859, his father Nicholas Rosewarne having emigrated to South Australia from Phillack, Cornwall, in 1857. The family moved to Wallaroo Mines in 1861. John Henry grew up there, became an apprentice and finally opened up his own business in 1882.

Top: Rosewarne's establishment between 1916 to 1920. By this time J. H. Rosewarne (who retired in 1917) had become a local identity, his firm dealing with everything from horseshoes to motor cars. Some conception of the extent and diversity of his activities can be gained from the fact that in 1906 he was employing no fewer than forty-two workmen.

Above: The Kadina Coffee Palace and Temperance Hotel, around 1911-12. It was originally the White Lion Hotel. Perhaps the change of name and function was evidence of the growing strength of the temperance movement in the years after 1900.

E.W. MARCHANT, PHOTOGRA
ROY·TEA

ENGINEER
MACHINIST
HODGES & COOK

Left, top: A humble cottage in Christie Street, Kadina, at the turn of the century. Although often described as Cornish, the simple, single-storeyed miners' cottages to be found on Yorke Peninsula and at Burra are more accurately 'colonial South Australian' in design. Their architecture was more reminiscent of perhaps Galway or the Western Isles than of Cornwall itself.

Left, middle: In this view, taken some seventy years ago, something of the activity and prosperity of Kadina's main shopping area, Taylor Street, is conveyed. In 1908 May Vivienne wrote that 'Kadina on a Saturday night is in great form. All the miners and their wives seem to come in to do their marketing, and have a bit of amusement into the bargain. Thousands of people flock the streets, the footpaths being crowded. The road takes the balance of the population, and it is quite a work of art to get through the crowd; but they are sober and good-humoured, and politely make way for the stranger if he is civil; if not, he may get some jostling'.

Left, bottom: Rosewarne's rivals. The premises of Messrs Hodge and Cook, engineers, wheelwrights, blacksmiths, machinists, as they appeared in 1912. The buggy featured in the photograph is no doubt one of their own creations.

Above: Taylor Street, Kadina, looking westwards towards Wallaroo Mines, about 1905. This view shows clearly the close proximity of Kadina to Wallaroo Mines. On the skyline at the left is the head frame of Office Shaft and the tall chimney of the power house; and all around the mines are scattered the employees' cottages.

Above: Football developed in the 1880s as a popular sport among the Cornish miners, and was one way in which local rivalries were played out. This photograph depicts the Wallaroo Mines Rovers Football Club in 1887, the year the team won theYorke Peninsula League Premiership.

Below: A miner's cottage of the better sort at Wallaroo Mines. The dressed stone in the front wall of the house, the verandah, and the well laid-out garden all point to an above-average level of affluence. And Father, second from the right, with his bowler hat and confident stance, looks suspiciously like a mine Captain - which would account for a higher level of income.

Left: A delightful study, probably in 1916, of two little girls standing near the main mine entrance to Wallaroo Mines. With the paraphernalia of industrial might all around, the photographer could still find time for more delicate themes.

Below: Wallaroo Mines, looking north-east in 1916. In the foreground is the Wallaroo Mines State School, with the pupils assembled in the playground. Immediately behind is Elder's pump engine, and in the distance is Kadina.

The Moonta Mines

The Moonta Mines have always managed to hog the limelight from all the other ventures on northern Yorke Peninsula, including the Wallaroo Mines. To some extent this can be explained by Oswald Pryor's tendency to concentrate on Moonta and by the highly-developed sense of local identity which grew up there. But more especially it can be attributed to the mystique created by and around Captain Henry Richard Hancock, the man who put Moonta Mines on the map. He ruled the Mines for nearly thirty-five years. He maintained a strict discipline but developed an advanced welfare policy. His determination to expand and exploit the mines sometimes brought him into conflict with more cautious directors and shareholders. But for the most part, decisions were left to Captain Hancock and the directors normally referred to him for his views and advice before embarking upon any new course of action. Captain Hancock became a legend in his own lifetime - famous not only in Australia, but also in Cornwall, America and South Africa - and as his fame spread so did that of the Moonta Mines.

Left, top: Henry Richard Hancock and his entourage of Cornish Captains and staff, Moonta Mines, 1866. Hancock is sitting front row, fourth from the left.

Left: Hughes's engine in the course of erection, around 1864-65. This was a 60-in (1.5-metre) cylinder pump engine, with a 10-ft (3-metre) stroke, built by Harvey & Co. of Hayle, Cornwall, in 1863. It worked twenty-four hours a day at Moonta for nearly sixty years until the mine's closure in 1923. The engine house was constructed by John Beaglehole, a builder in Ryan Street, Moonta, who was born in West Cornwall in 1831. Beaglehole came to South Australia in 1849, working at the Burra Burra Mine and on the Victorian goldfields before moving to Adelaide, then Wallaroo Mines, and finally Moonta. He was a founder of Moonta Wesleyan Sunday School, and was intimately involved in the Methodist Church until his death in 1910 *(photo reproduced by kind permission of Miss P. Minhard).*

Left, top: Richman's engine house and ore-concentrating plant, in its 1884 condition. Although not of typical Cornish design, this engine house is nevertheless similar to that erected at Hingston Down Mine, near Gunnislake, in East Cornwall. A 30-in (0.76-metre) engine was ordered for Richman's plant in 1868 and construction of the engine house completed in 1870. The engine was unusual in that it could be used winding, pumping, or stamping. The celebrated Warren-May jigger was developed for use at Richman's plant, and, with modifications effected by Captain Cowling (from Baldhu in West Cornwall), it formed the basis from which the famous Hancock Jigger evolved.

Left, middle: Elder's whim engine, about 1862-63. This photograph was taken only a matter of months after Wyatt drew his sketch, showing that the construction of the buildings and the erection of the engine has now been completed.

Left, bottom: A Beyer-Peacock 0-4-0 locomotive, the first railway engine to be used at the Moonta Mines.

Right, top: Cornish miners at Hughes's Shaft, 1894. As at Wallaroo Mines, the miners wear the typical Cornish helmets with candles attached.

Right: Bower's whim engine, about 1884. It was used for winding from both Green's and Fergusson's Shafts. When Prince Edward and Prince George (later King George V) visited the Moonta Mines in 1881 they were taken underground at Green's Shaft. On that occasion, Bower's engine was driven by a Cornishman named Thomas Trezise.

Left: Some of the staff of the Moonta Mines workshops, about 1890. The purpose of the photograph seems to be to portray the heavy-looking pneumatic drill in the foreground. These drills were used extensively at both Moonta and Wallaroo, and were developed in the well-equipped workshops at the mines.

Left, bottom: Warmington's Shaft in 1898. In the foreground, on either side of the railway lines, are two sunken bins associated with the adjoining Richman's plant. In the background can be seen Prankerd's engine house and boiler house.

Right: Pickey-boys in the ore-sorting plant at Moonta Mines, about 1913. The conveyor-belt in use here is evidence of a degree of mechanisation at the mines.

Below: Erecting a steel chimney stack at Richman's plant in 1908. The group of men on the right are dwarfed by the huge scale of the surrounding buildings and equipment.

BUTCHERS
W. CHAPPELL
BOOT-MAKER
MARSHALL & HERBERT
ELLERY
MR. W. CHAPPELL Snr
CLARA CHAPPELL
W. CHAPPELL Jnr
MR HERBERT

CHAPPELL'S
BOOT & SHOE WAREHOUSE

Settlements: Moonta and Moonta Mines

Like Kadina and Wallaroo Mines, a special, mutually-supportive relationship developed between the township of Moonta and the neighbouring miners' settlement of Moonta Mines. A great deal of rivalry existed between the two, but they combined to insist that, 'If you haven't been to Moonta (that is, the whole district) you haven't travelled'. Pryor suggested that perhaps the saying originated at Broken Hill in the 1880s, as a result of bantering between the Cousin Jacks from Bendigo and those from Moonta. But the phrase had been heard in the North American mining camps at an even earlier date, and was still current on the Western Australian goldfields at the turn of the century. As might be expected, the saying was not unknown in Cornwall itself.

Left, top: The premises of Marshall and Herbert, the butchers, and W. Chappell, the bootmaker, in George Street, around 1880.

Left: This view of George Street, Moonta, looking west, conveys much of the frontier atmosphere that existed in the town's early days. Shown are Solomon's Store (known as the 'Nimble Ninepence') *at left,* and the Institute (later the Friendly Society's Hall), *right.*

J. THOMAS
GROCER &c
1864
EAR

OTEL

IMPERIAL FIRE OFFICE
VALUATORS
D. ARCHIBALD & Co
AUCTIONEERS
AND ESTATE
AGENTS

Left, top: Ellen Street, Moonta, in its pre-1874 guise. The flat, sparsely-vegetated country visible at the end of the street gives some impression of the district's aridity and openness.

Left, middle: Moonta's heyday - George Street as it appeared between 1873 and 1885. Of particular interest is the gas lamp and lamp-lighter's ladder. Moonta had its own gasworks company from as early as 1873.

Left, bottom: David Archibald opened this shop at Moonta in 1881; and as well as being the local auctioneer he acted also as the valuator, estate agent, and insurance agent.

Above: A panoramic view down George Street before the turn of the century. Along the centre of the road is the tramway, leading out to Moonta Mines. All across the skyline is evidence of the mines themselves, from the huge tailings dumps on the left to Hughes's engine-house on the right.

Below: W.H Pengelly, blacksmith and wheelwright, one of the many Cornish mechanics on northern Yorke Peninsula. Research has failed to reveal the exact location of these premises, but they are thought to have been somewhere in the Moonta district and certainly within the confines of 'Little Cornwall' *(photo reproduced by kind permission of Miss P. Minhard).*

Above: A classic photograph of the Moonta Mines settlement, taken in 1897 from the ridge on Hamley Hill. Note the wooden slats on the roofs, and the abundance of picket fencing. The engine house in the background is that housing Hughes's pump engine.

Below: A charming portrait of a group of children outside an East Moonta cottage in 1883. The cottage, typical of those found on the mineral leases, belonged to a Cornish miner by the name of John Rowe.

Top: This cottage, one of the first to be erected at Moonta Mines, was built by a Cousin Jack called Peter Bowden. It was demolished over eighty years later on the death of Mary Bowden - its final occupant and last surviving member of the Bowden family.

Above: A Moonta Mines cottage following the advent of corrugated iron and the wireless - two inventions which considerably affected the lifestyle on the Mines settlements. Fifty years ago there were still several hundred of these cottages on the mineral leases, but today only a relative few remain.

Above: The Wilton home at Yelta (a settlement outside Moonta), around 1890 - evidently the establishment of a well-to-do family.

Top, centre: Kadina Road, Moonta, around 1900, looking towards the cemetery from the railway line. On the right are the substantial buildings of the 'Royal Hotel Sample Rooms', further evidence that the temperance movement did not have 100 per cent support in 'Little Cornwall'.

Top, right: The austere facade of the Moonta School of Mines. The left hand portion of the building was erected originally in 1866 as a Baptist chapel, but was reopened as the School of Mines in 1891. The right hand portion was added in the early 1900s to provide room for metallurgy and assaying laboratories.

Right: The popularity of local football matches is confirmed in this crowded view of the Moonta Showgrounds, thought to have been taken on 3 September 1921. The local Moonta team was always known popularly as the 'C.J.s' - short for Cousin Jacks.

OTEL SAMPLE ROOMS.

MOONTA SCHOOL OF MINES

The Smaller Mining Ventures

In addition to the Wallaroo and Moonta mines, there were numerous smaller workings on northern Yorke Peninsula, with heroic and euphonious names as Wheal Stuart, North Britain, Devon Consols, Wheal James, Vulcan, Royal, Prince of Wales, Nonspareil, Karoona, Albion, and Copper Valley. Although few were ever really successful, some lasted well into this century, while a number are of especial interest because they were 'nationalised' by John Verran's Labor Government and run as State enterprises. Verran was much criticised for this action - it was 'creeping socialism', or 'Cousin Jack favouritism', or a 'misallocation of resources' - but he parried all attacks with the response that he was a practical miner and therefore knew best. 'Honest John' acquired the Yelta, Paramatta, and Wandilta mines in 1911, and instigated prospecting on the Wallaroo Central and Wallaroo Extended setts. When accused in the House of Assembly of acquiring the properties without first seeking the opinion of qualified mining experts, Verran angrily replied, 'I am not going to officers who don't know as much about mining as I do'. Verran's purchases were much supported by the Peninsula folk (with the exception of the conservative *Kadina and Wallaroo Times*), and, following a considerable injection of capital, it appeared the venture might be a success. However, with the ultimate failure of Wallaroo and Moonta, it seems unlikely that the scheme would have worked in the long run. And a change of government in 1912 put an end to the experiment, for reasons that were partly economic but inevitably political.

Left, top: An unidentified working, probably in the Wallaroo Mines district, in the early 1860s. Of particular interest is the stone wall constructed around the whim and shaft in the right of the picture, which illustrates the considerable skill of the Cornish 'hedge builder'. (In Cornwall a 'hedge' is always made of stone and erected in the manner shown here) *(photo reproduced by kind permission of Miss P. Minhard).*

Left: Another very early mining scene - possibly at the same unidentified location. The profusion of plant suggests this is one of the larger workings *(photo reproduced by kind permission of Miss P. Minhard).*

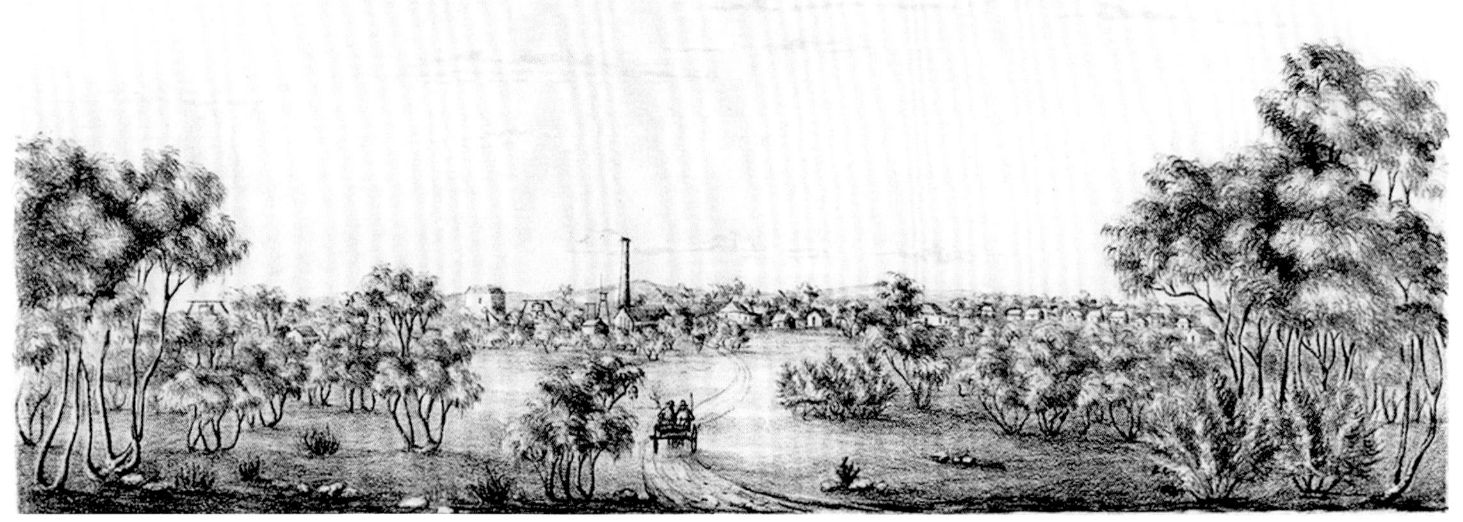

Above: Wyatt's sketch of the New Cornwall Mine, near Kadina, around 1863. The prospectus for this company was issued in February 1861, almost six months before the Moonta Mines were discovered. The sketch shows that development was rapid – two horse whims, an engine house, and numerous cottages can be discerned. The lode proved rich at surface, but failed at depth. Closure came finally as a result of an underground collapse, although there were later attempts at reworking the mine.

Below: Another sketch attributed to Wyatt, this time of the Matta Matta mine, near Kadina, about 1865. There is a horse whim, a small engine house, and an extensive supply of firewood. The building visible on the extreme right is apparently the celebrated Matta House, one-time home of Caroline Carleton, author of the 'Song of Australia'. Today, Matta House contains a National Trust museum.

Above, left: The Karkarilla Mine in 1906. Rich ore was discovered here in 1861, on the southern boundary of the Moonta leases, and a mine established. The engine and boiler houses were erected, but after a few years the property was abandoned. Later a new company acquired the mine and discovered a second lode situated a little farther west. The new western section was named the Hamley and operations concentrated there, the Karkarilla section soon being closed. In 1900 the Karkarilla was again opened, and the combined Hamley property continued as an independent concern until its absorption into the Wallaroo and Moonta Mining and Smelting Co. during the first World War.

Above, right: The directors and employees of the Copper Hill Mining Co., near Kadina. Clearly the Copper Hill was not a particularly rich venture, for it is not immediately obvious who are the directors and who are the employees!

Top: The Hamley Mine as it was in about 1916. From left to right are the chimney stack, boiler house, engine house, and crusher house. The rather ramshackle wooden structure in front of the crusher contains a Warren-May jigger for use in the treatment of low-grade ore. The Hamley was perhaps the most successful of the independent mines, and it has been suggested that its merger with the Wallaroo and Moonta Co. was deliberately engineered by the larger firm which allegedly flooded the Hamley's deepest and richest levels in order to destroy the mine's viability and thus make amalgamation inevitable. No firm evidence exists to support this claim, however.

Above: The Kurilla property, situated south-west of Wallaroo Mines. Originally worked in the early 1860s, the mine was abandoned and then restarted in 1868 under Captain Thomas Anthony. Born in Hayle, Cornwall, in 1831, Anthony worked for ten years as a pickey-boy in a local copper mine, became an apprentice blacksmith at sixteen, and by the age of twenty five was already a mine Captain. He arrived in South Australia in 1862 and went with his brother-in-law, John Hosking Trevorrow, to manage the Blinman Mine in the Flinders Ranges. In 1867 Anthony moved to Yorke Peninsula, and although he spent brief periods at both Yelta and Wallaroo Mines, he was associated with the Kurilla for more than a decade.

Top: The Paramatta Mine, discovered in 1866 in open country three kilometres north of Moonta by Joseph Lawn, Anthony Down and John Richards. The latter two came from Calstock in East Cornwall. They discovered copper while returning from a kangaroo-hunting trip. The mine was worked for some years and then abandoned. In 1899 it was reopened by a French company with Leigh Hancock (the second son of H. R. Hancock) as Captain. The photograph shows the mine in its 1900 to 1906 guise. From left to right are the vanner house, boiler and engine houses, crusher house and concentrating machinery, head frame, and blacksmith's shop and store. The mine was later taken over by the Verran Government of South Australia.

Above: The Yelta Mine, pictured in its 1911 condition, was opened up in 1861 on the northern boundary of the Moonta Mines, and worked successfully until 1878 when the low price of copper caused it to be closed. It was then worked sporadically until 1903 when it was acquired by the French company which also purchased the Paramatta. This company erected two blast furnaces for smelting and other modern plant, all of which came into the possession of the Verran Government in 1911.

MALCOLM & Co.
AUCTIONEERS

Settlements: Wallaroo and its Smelting Works

Situated on the western seaboard of Yorke Peninsula, Wallaroo was the maritime outlet for the mineral produce of 'Little Cornwall', and once vied with Port Pirie for the title of being the principal port on Spencer Gulf. For migrants journeying to the district by sea, Wallaroo was usually the point of disembarkation, and thus for many Cousin Jacks the town served as their first introduction to the northern Yorke Peninsula mining district. Apart from the harbour itself, the main feature of Wallaroo was its smelting works where ore from both the Wallaroo and Moonta mines was smelted. Originally, the works were erected and owned by the Wallaroo Mining Company, but in 1890 they became a part of the amalgamated firm. In the 1890s the smelting works were extended considerably so that by 1900 there were some thirty furnaces and twenty calcining kilns in operation. Machinery was also introduced to allow silver-lead ore from Broken Hill, and even gold from Western Australia, to be smelted. In the early 1900s there were further improvements, with modern blast furnaces and converters replacing the older plant, as well as sulphuric acid being produced as an important by-product of the smelting process. The smelting works continued in operation until 1923 when the closure of the local mines rendered them redundant. The smelting works were also responsible for Wallaroo' s sizeable Welsh element, a large number of Welshmen being brought to the area from the copper-smelting town of Swansea in South Wales. Many of these smelters were Welsh-speaking, and the Welsh language survived in the district for many years - a pleasant feature in an area with already an overwhelmingly Celtic flavour. Sadly, the Welsh tongue ultimately succumbed to pressure from 'official' English, as the Welsh community became outnumbered by the other ethnic groups on the peninsula. In the early years of this century many of the Wallaroo smelters bore Cornish names like Trelease, Chynoweth, Magor and Pascoe, whilst one had to search hard to find a Llewellyn or a Gruffydd.

Left, top: An early view of Wallaroo West Side, showing something of the barren, treeless, and rather hostile environment in which the town was created. Note the railway trucks standing in the sidings in the centre left of the photograph, and the station building a little to their right.

Left, middle: Hughes Street in 1910. Compared with the preceding view, this photograph, taken at a somewhat later date, shows Wallaroo as a substantial, well-populated, and important township . In the background, on the extreme right, masts of two ships moored at Wallaroo jetty can just be seen.

Left, bottom: The appropriately-named Prince of Wales Hotel as it appeared around 1895. Also visible are the stockyards of Malcolm & Co., auctioneers at the local Wallaroo market.

STATIONER &c
GEO E. PRITCHARD. M.P.S.
STATIONER.
TONKIN'S.
TEA ROOMS

Left, top: The shop names visible in this photograph (taken sometime between 1907 and 1911) attest to Wallaroo's predominantly Celtic background - Prichard is a common Welsh surname, whilst Tonkin and Hocking are typically Cornish.

Left, middle: The smelting works as they appeared during the 1870s. Although already an extensive establishment (some twelve chimney stacks can be discerned), the works are still in an embryonic stage when compared with the photograph showing the works in their 1920 condition. The massive chimney, situated to the right of the white-washed buildings, is still standing today and bears the inscription 'W. W. H. 1861', a reference to the Scottish sea-captain, Walter Watson Hughes, on whose property copper was first discovered in 1859.

Left, bottom: The smelting works in 1920. On the extreme left are the copper storerooms, while in the centre stands the original chimney stack with the copper refinery alongside. The white building on the right, with its various tiers and towers, is the sulphuric acid plant. The acid produced by the smelting works was sold to the neighbouring Wallaroo Phosphate Company for use in the manufacture of superphosphate, a fertiliser product used extensively in the agricultural industry.

Above: A startling photograph, apparently taken from the top of one of the stacks, of the smelting works about 1910. The sea, although not quite visible in this view, lies not many metres to the left. The works were built almost on the foreshore.

Above: Charging the refinery furnace, about 1914 to 1920. Slabs of rough copper are being fed into the refinery by a 'paddle' - the long instrument visible in the photograph, on the front of which is a paddle-shaped attachment for holding the slabs.

Below: A 'dark satanic mill' if ever there was one! Shafts of light pierce the gloominess of the works, as blister copper is poured from the converter vessels into a series of moulds arranged on tramway trucks. This photograph was taken sometime between 1914 and 1920.

Above: 'Jack Biggs's coffee pot', an antiquated 0-4-0 locomotive, seen here in use at the smelting works in the early 1900s. The funnel was hinged to allow the engine to enter sheds whose doorways were lower than the standard loading gauge.

Below: The Wallaroo Regatta, about 1914. The regatta was one of the high-spots in the local sporting calendar, and literally hundreds of people from all over the peninsula thronged the jetty and foreshore to watch the various events *(photo reproduced by permission of Miss P. Minhard).*

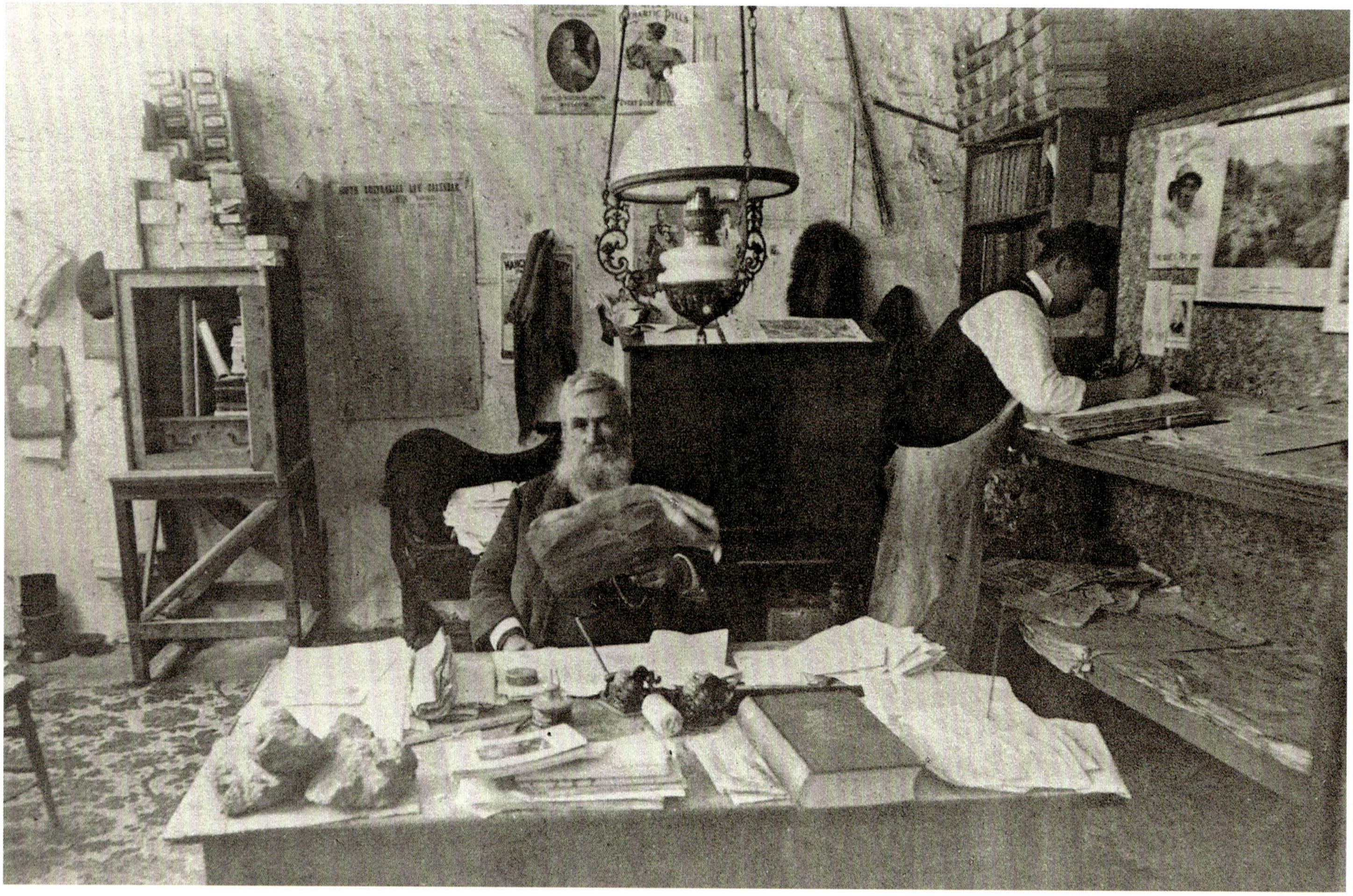

Above: The original premises in Bagot Street of the *Wallaroo Times*, founded in 1865. The gentleman seated at the table is co-owner and editor of the newspaper, David Taylor, who came out from Scotland with his brother in the early days of the colony's existence *(photo reproduced by permission of Miss P. Minhard).*

Left: An interesting study of the Wallaroo Inn, around 1891-96. Ellen Waters was probably a Cornishwoman, Waters being the typically Cornish form of the patronymic name Walters.

Above: Andy Appleton and his billy-goat cart in the early 1900s. Goats, as any devotee of Oswald Pryor cartoons will know, were a feature of the 'Little Cornwall' district. Although goats could become a severe nuisance, they could also be put to good uses. As well as providing fresh milk for many local families, they were ideal for pulling small carts of the type Master Appleton is using here to collect firewood.

Right: The premises of W. H. May & Sons of Wallaroo. The May family came from the Cornish parish of Perranzabuloe and arrived in South Australia in 1858. Settling first at the Burra Burra Mine, the family soon moved to Yorke Peninsula where Frederick May - at the age of 23 - became chief engineer on the Wallaroo Mines. In 1875 William Henry May opened his foundry at Wallaroo in conjunction with another Cornishman, Stephen Tonkin. Tonkin left the partnership in 1881, leaving May to run the establishment alone until 1904 when he brought his three sons into the firm. The foundry played an important role in the development of the local farming industry, with such inventions as the 'Little Marvel' harvester and the 'Twin Skim' plough.

Cousin Jack Underground

D. Bradford Barton, the celebrated Cornish mining historian, notes in his *Historic Cornish Mining Scenes Underground* that 'photographs taken underground on metal mines are rarities . . .' and stresses in particular the scarcity of scenes depicting Cornish miners at work. The following collection of photographs, taken underground at Wallaroo Mines in the period 1890 to 1923, is thus of considerable historical value and importance; they illustrate not only conditions in a large Australian metal mine at the turn of the century, but also Cousin Jack engaged in the trade for which he had won world renown - mining. These photographs convey, too, something of the frightening, almost surreal, atmosphere of a mine deep underground. Anyone who has ever been down a mine will not easily forget the experience - the unnerving descent in the cage, the strange and powerful smells that are encountered, the humidity, the slipperiness and grime, the inky-blackness broken only by the light on the helmet, and the peculiar sensation of walking along a level or climbing a ladder when one has no conception of where are the vertical and horizontal planes. For the miner, familiarity with this environment reduces its impact and effect. But nothing can detract from the dangerous and strenuous nature of the miner's work.

Left: A double-deck man skip, capable of holding six men in each compartment, at one of the shaft plats (platforms), about 1914-18. Although these skips were hardly comfortable and could sometimes be dangerous (for instance, William Hobb was killed by putting his head out of a descending skip at the 11 5 fathom level and dashing it against áthe side of Taylor's Shaft, Moonta Mines, in 1893), they were certainly a great advance on the use of ladders, or even man engines. The latter, developed in Cornwall at the Tresavean Mine, were little more than pump rods with standing steps attached, and were also employed at the Wallaroo Mines. There was, for example, a man engine installed in 1876 in the old Hughes's engine shaft.

Left: Erecting main level timbers at the 2430 feet (405 fathoms or 741 metres) level, about 1917–18. Owing to the fact that much of the ground encountered on Yorke Peninsula was considerably softer than that in Cornwall, the Wallaroo Mines were more closely timbered than their Cornish counterparts. The Moonta Mines, however, were situated in a zone of hard rock and timbering there was much lighter than at Wallaroo. Until the regime of H. Lipson Hancock, all depths in the peninsula mines were measured in fathoms – as was the usual Cornish practice – but the standard unit of the foot was later adopted as part of the general modernisation programme.

Below: Stoping underground, using pneumatic drills, in 1916. 'Stoping', a term of Cornish origin, is the miner's word to describe the actual process of extracting the ore. The drill in the right of the picture is supported by a vertical pole known as a stretcher.

Top: The main level at 205 feet (93 metres), west of Young's Shaft. The miner pushing the truck along the level is tramming ore to the shaft plat, and the timberman on the left (note his saw) is about to climb up a 'winze' (a short shaft connecting underground workings but which does not reach the surface). Again, the closeness and orderly nature of the timbering is unlike that found in most Cornish mines.

Above: Emptying truck loads of ore into shaft ore bins, whence the ore gravitates into dirt skips to enable it to be hauled to surface.

Left: A 'telescope' rock drill in use underground in a stope situated near either Young's or Taylor's shaft, about 1914.

Above: The two miners in the top right hand corner (with the drill) are apparently preparing a place in which to secure a main level timber. However, there appears to be such a concentration and diversity of activity in so small a space that this photograph gives the impression that it could have been posed.

Far left: Replacing timbers, again in the '2340 feet' level. Note the various implements and objects placed along the right-hand wall - a Cornish shovel, a saw, a bar or length of pipe, a jerry can, and another shovel.

Left: It is not clear whether this photograph of timbermen at work was taken at Moonta or at Wallaroo. Although described as being at Moonta Mines, it is probably part of the Wallaroo Mines collection.

Left, bottom: A classic photograph of a shaft plat, taken in 1916. In the right-hand section of the shaft is a ladderway - one miner is climbing upwards towards the next level, while another can be seen preparing to descend. One retired miner recalled that on Sundays, when only a few men were underground, the whim engines would not be manned and thus miners had to climb all the way to surface up ladderways, instead of riding in the man skips. On the ground, near the ladderway, is a box containing a supply of Burford's Mining Candles - the miner's source of light underground.

Below: The underground electric pumps in Taylor's Shaft, soon after their installation in 1905. The date '20/8/95' was clearly written in error, and no doubt should read 20/8/05. To be in charge of the electric pumps was generally considered a soft job by the underground workmen, although there were occasional instances of electrocution. The lighted miners' candles can be seen clearly in this photograph; the miner in the left foreground has spare candles attached to his jacket.

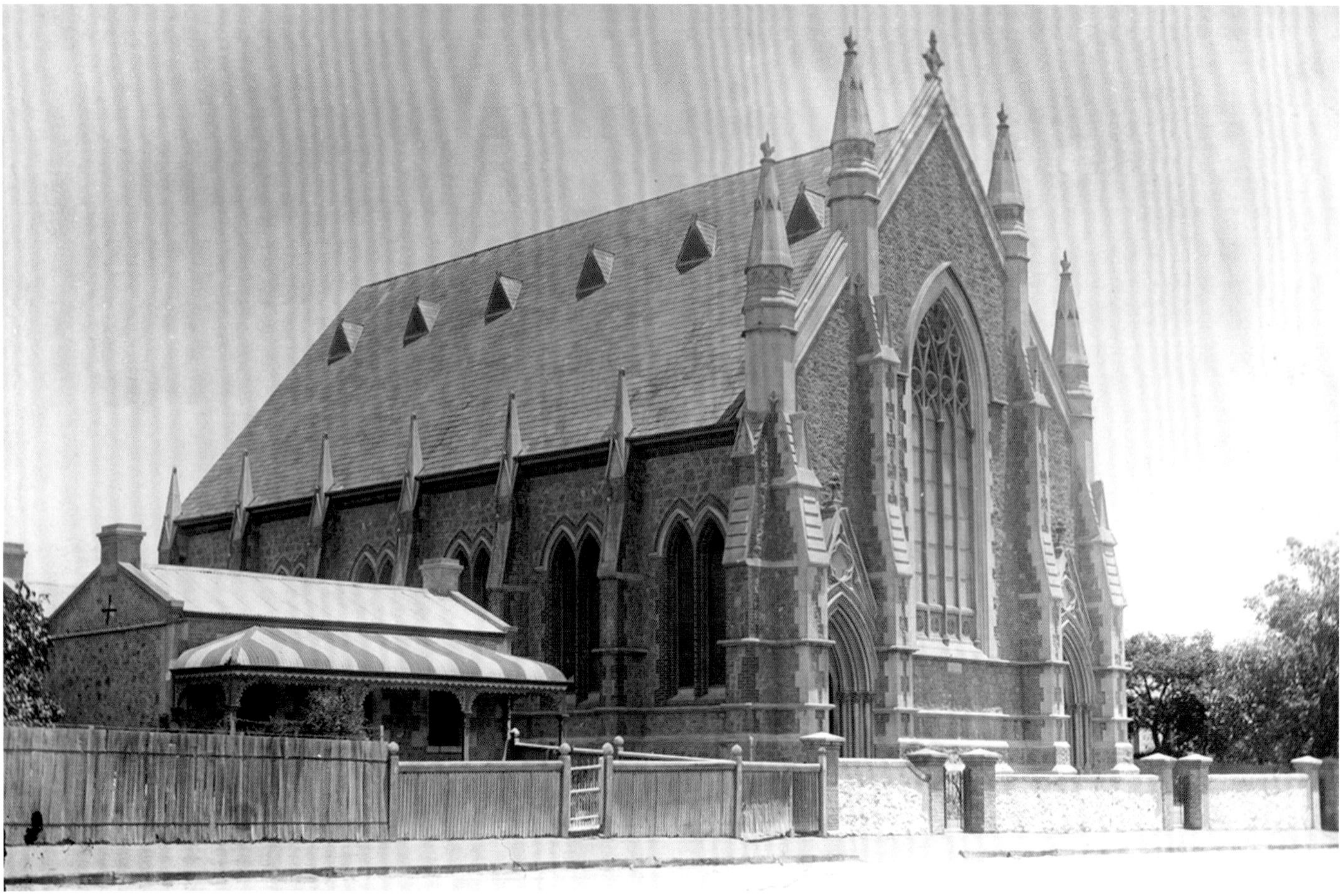

Chapels, Banners and Bands

In 'Little Cornwall', recreation, religion, and politics were often inextricably entwined. The tea-treat or temperance parade would be conducted in carnival mood, but with the deeper significance never forgotten. Trade union officials were nearly always Methodist class leaders or local preachers - their industrial and political activities being for them merely a practical extension of their Christian convictions. Brass bands were formed partly for their own sake, for the sheer pleasure of making music, but often they existed in association with a particular chapel or union branch, and could be seen heading the parades of the numerous organisations which existed in the district. The strength and purpose of religious nonconformity on northern Yorke Peninsula is evident in the words of the Reverend D. C. Harris who preached to a congregation of 1200 people at Moonta Mines Methodist Church in June 1904, following a march staged by the local Orange Lodge. He declared, 'The work of Protestantism would not be finished and the Orange Institution would not survive the need ot its existence until the Church of Rome came back to the New Testament and the sway of the Papacy was at an end'. Nevertheless, before the union of the various denominations in 1901, Methodist solidarity was not all it might have been. There was considerable rivalry between the different sects and the different chapels. At Moonta, for example, a spirit of competition existed between the Wesleyans (tending to be middle-class, township dwellers) and the other denominations. The Primitive Methodists had their own internal problems which led, at one point, to blows being exchanged between rival groups at East Moonta and ultimately, in 1880, to the secession of the Moonta Circuit from the South Australia District. The rift was healed by the creation of two new districts, those of Moonta and Adelaide, but full reunification was not achieved until 1888 when the South Australia District was restored.

Left, top: Robert Street Methodist Church,Moonta, as it appeared in the 1920s. Built at a cost of £4000, and opened in 1874 as a Wesleyan chapel, its gradiose Victorian Gothic style contrasts with the austere, classical designs of the Primitive Methodist and Bible Christian chapels.

Left: The Brass Band of the Amalgamated Miners' Association, Kadina Branch , winners of the Yorke Peninsula banding contest held on 27 December 1913. A Miners' Association was formed at Moonta in the early 1870s, and in the 1880s it was reconstituted as a branch of the A.M.A., with other branches being formed at Wallaroo and Kadina. The A.M.A. itself was later absorbed into the Australian Workers' Union.

Top: A Sunday School anniversary parade forms up, complete with the chapel band, at East Moonta Methodist Church, about 1910. At first sight the banner frame held aloft seems empty, but in fact the banner has been blown high by a gust of wind.

Above: A procession in Graves Street, Kadina, in celebration of the 'Eight Hours System'. The leading banner is that of the A.M.A., Moonta Branch, while that following sports the device of the Wallaroo Wharfside Workers.

Right, top: Erected in the early 1870s as the Moonta Bible Christian chapel, this building was later purchased by the Church of Christ and was in their possession at the time this photograph was taken about 1918.

Right: The superbly-named Copper City Brass Band, photographed in its home town of Kadina in 1909.

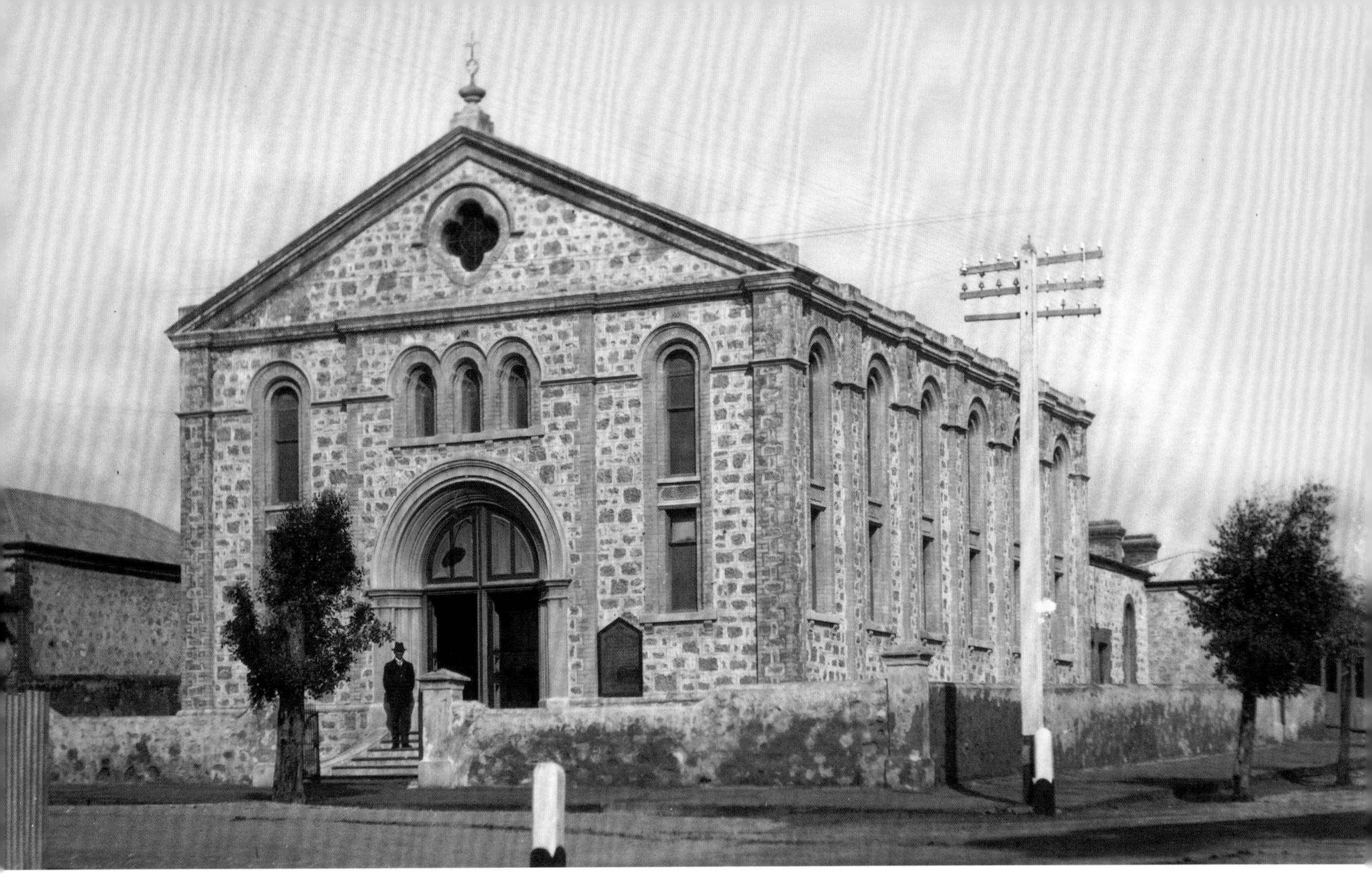

Left: Yelta Wesleyan Church, erected in 1873 and demolished in 1931, was typical of many, small unpretentious chapels built all over South Australia in the great days of Methodism but which have long since disappeared. With its simplistic facade and random-stone construction, Yelta Church bore a strong similarity to the numerous wayside chapels to be found all over Cornwall.

Below: A float prepared by Hollands Brothers for a Labor Day procession at Moonta in the early years of this century. Surprisingly, the Burford's product being advertised is not miners' candles but soap.

Right: Blood and Fire! It would have been difficult for the Salvation Army to have devised a more apt or evocative slogan than the one shown here adorning its barracks at Wallaroo; photograph taken about 1900.

Below: The Wallaroo Mines Federal Band, about 1910. After the federation of the six colonies to form the Commonwealth of Australia in 1901, various organisations incorporated the word 'federal' into their names to celebrate the coming of nationhood. This, presumably, was how this particular band achieved its name.

BUNYIP
NAPTHA

Left, top: The Kadina Band in procession, Kadina, sometime in the penod 1910 to 1920. The leading horseman is cleverly attired as a Bengal Lancer, bringing a touch of the Indian sub-continent to the streets of 'Little Cornwall'.

Left, middle: The celebrated Moonta Mines Methodist Sunday School (ex-Primitive Methodist chapel) in 1911. The weatherboard huts to the left of the stone building are all part of the Sunday School, and were erected after 1905 as part of the American-inspired Rainbow System adopted by H. Lipson Hancock - then Superintendent of the school. The Rainbow System, explained by Hancock in his various books on the subject, was an authoritarian, regimented method of Sunday School teaching. It had a rigid code of behaviour - imposed on all pupils who ranged from infancy to twenty-three years and upwards. There were ten grades, from the 'Cradle Roll' to the 'Home Grade' for those too ill or aged to attend the classes. The actual Rainbow course of instruction consisted of 100 lessons which investigated every facet of the Bible, culminating in Lesson 100, 'The Call of China'.

Left, bottom: The well-equipped Kadina Salvation Army Band, about 1919.

Above: The formation of bands was not an activity restricted to adults alone, as evidenced by this illustration of the Kadina Primary School Band, about 1913-15.

The Years of Change

Fortunately, the closure of the mines in 1923 did not lead to the total destruction of the local community, for by then Yorke Peninsula had developed as an important farming district, As early as the 1870s, Cornish miners had begun selecting land in the locality of the mines, and the following decades were characterised by the movement of Cornish miner-turned-farmers southwards down the peninsula and north-eastwards towards Bute and Snowtown. Rendering the land fit for farming was no easy task, as Charles Wesley Bowden recalled: 'My father, and others from Cornwall, had to do the job properly or not at all. But I don't think they had any Black Mallee roots to contend with in the Old Country'.

Despite the difficulties, farming, particularly wheat-growing, was established in the area, and Kadina developed in the twentieth century as an important regional centre to serve the needs of local farmers. The port of Wallaroo became the export-point for the locality's grain produce. Today, the mighty silos at Wallaroo attest to the area's continuing prosperity. Moonta, too, survived as a regional centre, and is now the focal point of an expanding tourist industry. Undoubtedly, the growth in tourism has been one consequence of the interest provoked by the Kernewek Lowender Cornish Festival. 'Kernewek Lowender' - meaning literally, in the Cornish language, 'Cornish Happiness' - has a distinctly Cornish flavour. There is, for example, the 'Fer Trev' (village fair), the 'Fer Kernewek' (Cornish fair), and 'swanky' can be purchased in the local hotels. The Furry Dance - performed to the time honoured Cornish tune - wends its way through the streets of Kadina, and the black and white cross of St Piran (the Cornish 'national flag') flies proudly from public buildings and flagpoles in the district.

Left, top: Moonta Extended Mine in 1930 or 1931. Although the principal mining operations ceased in 1923, there were sporadic attempts during the inter-war years to rework parts of the mines or to retreat wastes. There were several 'one man shows', where individuals worked sections of ground on tribute, and occasionally there were larger enterprises involving more heavy injections of capital. The Moonta Extended was worked by the syndicate shown here.

Left: 'Scatterin' the bal'. After the mine closures in 1923, the mining plant was meticulously and efficiently dismantled for sale - a mammoth operation in itself. In this scene (about 1924) the last Cornish boiler is being removed from Wallaroo Mines.

Left, top: An attempted reworking of Bennett's Shaft, Moonta Mines, in 1931-32. The abandoned Hughes's engine house stands forlornly in the background.

Left, middle: Smith's Shaft, Moonta Mines, during the attempted reworking in 1931-32.

Left, bottom: Although bullock teams belong to the lore of Australia's nineteenth-century pioneering era, they in fact survived in use well into this century. In this view, an eighteen-bullock team is seen at work on Cliff Rodda's farm, near Kadina, during the 1920s.

Below: Despite a certain degree of depopulation and a high level of unemployment during the inter-war years, progress did not entirely ignore 'Little Cornwall'. Here, the first broad-gauge train, hauled by an S Class 4-4-0 locomotive of the South Australian Railways, is seen leaving Moonta for Adelaide on 1 August 1927.

Bottom: Workers recovering precipitates at the Moonta Copper Recovery Company's works in 1937.

Top: It is not often realised that square-rigged sailing ships remained in revenue-earning service until the second World War, the last one to visit Wallaroo arriving in 1939. In this view of grain ships at Wallaroo in the 1930s, tall ships are still very much in evidence. The ships (both sail and steam) tied-up in front of the jetty are, from left to right, the ***Archibald Russell***, the ***Isleworth*** and the ***Rio Diamanti***. Those behind are the ***Abraham Rydberg***, the ***Deepal***, and the ***Penang***.

Above: The crowds surge along George Street during the 'Back to Moonta' celebrations, 17 September 1927. The mines had only been closed for four years, but already 'Little Cornwall' and its Cornish heritage had achieved legendary status throughout the country.

Right, top: The Cornish Furry Dance, being performed at the Fer Kernewek, and led by members of the Cornish Association of South Australia *(photo by courtesy of Publicity Branch, Premier's Department).*

Right: The leading float of the Fer Kernewek (Cornish fair) procession at the 1973 Kernewek Lowender Festival. Historical authenticity and the festival's Cornish atmosphere were achieved largely through the research work of Roslyn Paterson who, for her efforts, was created a Bard of the Gorseth Kernow (Cornish Gorsedd) - an important Cornish cultural body, linked with the Gorseddau of Wales and Brittany. Hundreds of other local residents have also worked tirelessly and well to ensure the continued success of the Kernewek Lowender *(photo by courtesy of the Publicity Branch, Premier's Department).*